"As she shares her personal life's journey, which include various ups and plenty of downs, and also identifies corresponding human experiences of some of the most notable bible characters of all-time, we find that Kristen McNulty is not short of company. Each true story she shares reinforces the fact that nobody, from those that lived in biblical times to each of us on earth right now, gets through the human experience without some suffering. But often, as she deftly points out, the natural human response is to struggle through life on our own because surrendering seems more of an act of giving up rather than one that allows good to find its way to us.

And so, as in these pages, the reoccurring questions are posed again and again throughout time: why do we often choose suffering over surrendering; doubt over trust; vulnerability over security? Why when the God of the Universe, God who is love personified, offers not only to take away our burdens, but also to give us a life filled with hope and a future? In Closed Doors, *Kristen gives her readers invaluable perspectives that can help them choose "doors" in life that can lead to a life filled with peace, security, joy, fulfillment..."*

IRENE DUNLAP
Co-author, *Chicken Soup for the Soul* book series
Author, *TRUE, Volumes I and II*

CLOSED DOORS

Finding God and Purpose
in the Unexpected

KRISTEN MCNULTY

Closed Doors: Finding God and Purpose in the Unexpected
Copyright © 2014 by Kristen McNulty

All rights reserved. No portion of this book may be reproduced, store in a retrieval system, or transmitted in any form or by any means – electronic, mechanical, photocopy, recording, scanning, or other – except for brief quotations in critical reviews or articles, without the prior written permission of the author.

Published by Paid In Full Publication

Titles may be purchased in bulk for education, business, fundraising, or sales promotional use. For information, please email specialmarkets@paidinfullpublication.com

Library and Archives Canada Cataloguing in Publication

McNulty, Kristen, 1983-, author
    Closed doors: finding God and purpose in the unexpected / Kristen McNulty.

Includes bibliographical references and index.
Issues in print and electronic formats.
ISBN 978-0-9939795-0-7.—ISBN 978-0-9939795-1-4 (epub)

    1. Life change events—Religious aspects—Christianity. 2. Suffering—Religious aspects—Christianity. 3. Adjustment (Psychology)—Religious aspects—Christianity. 4. Christian life. I. Title.

BV4905.3.M33 2014   248.8'6   C2014-907642-8
                                            C2014-907643-6

Unless otherwise indicated, scripture quotations are taken from the Holy Bible, New Living Translation, copyright ©1996, 2004, 2007, 2013 by Tyndale House Foundation. Used by permission of Tyndale House Publishers, Inc., Carol Stream, Illinois 60188. All rights reserved.

Scripture quotations marked (NIV) are taken from the Holy Bible, New International Version®, NIV®. Copyright © 1973, 1978, 1984, 2011 by Biblica, Inc.™ Used by permission of Zondervan. All rights reserved worldwide. www.zondervan.com The "NIV" and "New International Version" are trademarks registered in the United States Patent and Trademark Office by Biblica, Inc.™

Some names in this book have been changed to protect the privacy of the individuals involved.

Cover & Interior Design: Gnibel.com

Printed in the United States of America

DEDICATION

*To my mom, Pauline McNulty,
whose prayers have sustained me,
whose guidance has shaped me
and whose love touches everyone she meets.*

Table of Contents

Introduction ix

1. And It Begins
Facing disappointment and finding your bearings afterwards 1

2. Did I Take a Wrong Turn?
Learning that closed doors can be a part of God's plan 9

3. So I'm in the Desert, Now What?
Blooming where you are planted and trusting in God's timing ... 21

4. When We Can't Drive in Reverse
Owning up to your mistakes and receiving grace 29

5. Throw It To See If It'll Stick
Escaping the fear of failure and instead walking in faith 41

6. Ideal Destination or Idol?
*Discovering the difference between dreams and idols
that enslave* 51

7. You're Still Here
Identifying your purpose and living out each day to the fullest ... 63

8. Results Can Be Deceiving
Uncovering your gifts and rethinking how to be using them 71

9. For Such a Time as This
Remaining faithful even when in unfamiliar territory 83

10. Surrendering Your Isaac
Offering to God what you hold dearest even when you don't understand 91

11. The Darkness Before The Dawn
Embracing truth in the midst of darkness and lies 99

12. Find Healing At the Wall
Hitting rock bottom and finding hurt can bring true healing .. 111

13. Waiting for Sunday
Encountering delays and discovering their place in the plan 121

14. Waking Up in Babylon
Recognizing that closed doors and detours are often the destination 129

15. The God Who Goes Before Us
Following the God who goes ahead and makes a way 137

16. Last Chapter Of The Book, Not Your Life Story
Embracing every moment in your story and obeying God's leading 143

Bibliography 149
Acknowledgments 151
About the Author 153

Introduction

Closed doors and detours in our lives usually hit us by surprise. We walk confidently through life, thinking we're heading in one direction, but then it happens: an illness, the loss of a job, financial problems, the breakdown of a relationship, or unexpected circumstances that closes a door and sends us in a completely different direction.

How did this happen? Where will this road take me? Did I do something wrong to end up here?

All of these questions circle in our minds and answers seem a long way off.

This wasn't the way I thought life was supposed to work out. Not that I was so naive that I thought life would always be perfect, but I did picture my days here on earth as a scene out of the Footprints story. Walking in a straight line along the shore towards a destination, with trouble inevitably coming up along the way, but being okay because Jesus would be there to carry me.

The reality is quite different. Not that Jesus isn't there to carry us, but in my life and I'm sure yours, the footprints don't follow a straight line. Instead there is a great deal of back in forth, some patterns of endless circles and plenty of zig zags along the way.

Wouldn't it be nice if life could just be one straight line where our destination was defined and the possibility of surprise twists along the way would be completely removed? While it's a nice thought its not very realistic which is why I'm writing this book and something about it's title connected with you to make you want to pick it up.

The truth of the matter is life is messy. Our life stories don't always have the endings we anticipated and sometimes it's easy to wonder if the guy holding the pen is playing some sort of joke on us. It's a life where point A doesn't necessarily lie on the path to point B and often the journey to get there takes us on unexpected stops along the way. It's a life that can feel like a storm and a desert at the exact same time. It's a life where doors close and others don't necessarily open. It's also a life where we are not given a personalized and clearly defined roadmap to follow.

Nonetheless it is our lives. These are the stories that have been written for us, the set of circumstances that we've been given to deal with. And in that, while we know that there may be no way out of the unexpected, there is purpose in it.

Finding God and purpose in the unexpected is what this book is about. It's not a seven step manual to open any closed door you come across. It is, however, an accompaniment for your journey.

We begin at the moment where everything changes.

CHAPTER ONE

And It Begins

*"Do not look back and grieve over the past,
for it is gone; and do not be troubled about the future,
for it has not yet come. Live in the present, and make it
so beautiful that it will be worth remembering."*
— IDA SCOTT TAYLOR

We remember many defining moments in our lives: births, marriages, deaths, separations, graduations. These things have something in common: they are a major turning point that either marks the beginning of one journey or the end of another.

The same goes with "the moment". I'm sure you remember it clearly. Maybe you were at work, at the park, at home, or talking with friends, but it happened. It was the moment in time when you realized you had veered off course and were no longer heading in the direction you hoped to be, in the timeline you were aiming for. In that one moment you recognized the perfect picture you had for your future was taking on a different shape and you were powerless to do anything about it.

Maybe for years you wanted to get a certain job, you went to school, you worked hard, you did your best and you were faithful to God all the way through. Nonetheless suddenly a door is slammed shut and you're told it could be many more years before that job is yours, if ever.

Or maybe you had your life picture all laid out encompassing marriage, kids, and nights spent in the glow of their love like a scene out of some cheesy chick flick. However you find yourself in your middle-aged years and still single. Mr. or Mrs. Right has not come knocking and with each day that is being marked off the calendar, you're one step closer to seeing your dream going up in flames.

Or it could be that you've felt called by God to do something. Start a ministry, take a missions trip, pursue a different career or whatever it might be that you were absolutely sure God was calling you to. But suddenly circumstances strike: a job loss, an illness, family problems, financial difficulty, and that door is suddenly locked tight. Leaving you unsure when, or if, it will ever be opened again.

Whatever your story is, whatever your disappointment might be, we all can remember "the moment" and that can be the start of a very depressing season in our lives.

For me "the moment" came in June of 2007. Before the moment came, life was good. After spending many months battling a major illness that came as a result of surgery went wrong, I had returned to school and was working on my degree by correspondence. I had been offered and had accepted my dream job. My radio program, the MAD Christian Radio Show, and the young adult ministry I led was going quite well and for the first time in my life I felt like I clearly knew where I was heading. Looking ahead, I was quite excited for the possibilities and opportunities.

However life didn't stay so neat and planned out. Where I thought my health problems were done and behind me, they had only just begun. I developed a sleeping disorder and battled with insomnia that was so bad I was only getting a few hours of sleep a night. Being stubborn, I didn't let that stop me. No matter how tired I was or how much pain I was in (another lovely side effect), I kept on going with school, work, ministry, and life. I did not want to give in to this thing that was consuming my life, I wasn't about to let my dreams and my plans be sidetracked by something so seemingly random — as if I had a choice.

"The moment" slapped me in the face in June 2007. After many months of pushing and pushing and pushing, hoping that things would get better, yet unintentionally making it worse, I crashed. I remember it like it was yesterday. I had just written three exams that I had no clue if I would would pass or fail as my short-term memory had disappeared along with my good nights sleep and I was fried. I had pushed so hard yet I knew that I had hit that wall where I couldn't push anymore. Something had to give and with something having to give, it meant there was no way to keep my crazy plans on track.

As I informed the school of my decision not to return for the summer semester and I started saying no and cutting things out of my schedule, I remember feeling such a profound sense of disappointment. After all, these things that I was a part of weren't random occurrences or roles I took lightly. Instead I had prayed about them many times and saw one door open after another, allowing me to continue with them. To walk away like that left me feeling like a complete and utter failure.

In another moment, a moment of wisdom, I was told that if God wanted me doing all of those things, He would have either healed me of my sickness or given me the energy to do the tasks at hand. While that was a way to avoid feeling so responsible for what I viewed as a shortcoming (as in I just couldn't hack it), it didn't take away the discouragement I felt of having my footprints life story taking a sharp turn away from where I thought I was going.

Did this mean I was never going back to school? Was all of that work really for nothing? What about my dream job? Was I going to be able to keep up with that, or would it too be ripped away? Would my ministries suffer? Would I find help to lighten the load or was I going to have to throw everything I valued aside?

These questions plagued me like crazy and answers weren't always so forthcoming.

To say I was not a happy camper after "the moment" is an understatement. Turns out though, I'm not the only one.

In the book of Jonah we find a guy I can relate to for a many reasons, but the part of his life story that resonates with me the most comes from the line that utters,

> *"This change of plans greatly upset Jonah, and he became very angry." (Jonah 4:1)*

We find this line after the story is told about Jonah not listening to God and thus finding himself in the belly of a whale. After his unique aquatic experience, Jonah finally did what God asked of him. He went to Nineveh and told the people that they had 40 days before God was going to destroy their city. Message finally delivered, Jonah had his plan laid out in front of him. He was going to leave the city and watch in the rearview mirror as it went up in smoke. Instead, the people of Nineveh put a monkey wrench in Jonah's plans when they heard his message and rather than scoffing, they repented. Where many a person might rejoice over their repentance, Jonah got angry. Not due to of the state of their hearts per say, but because he knew the change of the state of their hearts could change the fate of the city. Thus, what Jonah thought was going to happen would be thrown out the window,

> *"So he [Jonah] complained to the Lord about it: 'Didn't I say before I left home that you would do this, Lord? That is why I ran away to Tarshish! I knew that you are a merciful and compassionate God, slow to get angry and filled with unfailing love. You are eager to turn back from destroying people. Just kill me now, Lord! I'd rather be dead than alive if what I predicted will not happen." (Jonah 4:2-3)*

To Jonah, this unexpected change in plans was worse for him to face than being dead. That's a pretty severe reaction, but it's one we can identify with. It is very easy to slip into a state of anger, desperation and despair when things in our lives don't go quite like we wanted them to.

Is that where you are finding yourself now? The change has been made. The destiny you had in your mind has been altered. And now you find yourself feeling angry and dejected.

If so, you're not alone. Jonah felt that way. Even Elijah, one of the heroes of the faith, felt the same way when his journey took an unexpected twist.

The feelings are real and they aren't something that we can just turn off. God created us to experience a wide range of emotions, from joy to grief and everything in between. Whenever we try to deny any of those feelings we're doing ourselves a disservice.

Some Christians feel sheepish to admit they are disappointed with where life has led them. Tracing back, I believe, to a fear people are going to look at them like they are a weaker believer if they are disappointed. But that only goes to show what a messed up idea we have of strength. True strength in character admits when it's weak, when it's broken and when it's feeling like it can't go on like this.

Turning to look at the story of Elijah in more detail, we pick up the story after he had just defeated the prophets of Baal and called down consuming fire from heaven to light up an alter in the ultimate display of God's existence and all-consuming power. Where many of us would assume a person in this situation would find themselves on some sort of emotional high after an event like that, the Bible tells us that Elijah was, to borrow a phrase from Anne of Green Gables, in the depths of despair. Elijah even pleads with God to end his life,

> *"Then he went on alone into the desert, traveling all day. He sat down under a solitary broom tree and prayed*

> *that he might die. 'I have had enough LORD,' he said. 'Take my life, for I am no better than my ancestors who have already died.'"* (1 Kings 19:4)

You see while Elijah was obedient to God and saw Him move in an out of this world kind of way, Elijah still came face to face with the realization that life was not going to go as planned afterwards. Elijah assumed he was finally in the clear after that display, but instead found out that he was still a wanted man who would have to live on the run. Instead of facing that challenge head on, Elijah asked God to take his life. That is despair and that is something that none of us are immune from experiencing.

While I hope you haven't been so deep in despair that you've asked God to take your life, feeling despair, discouragement and disappointment are very natural feelings which can accompany a change in our plans. I think though what is important for us to learn from the story of Elijah is God's response to Elijah's pain. God doesn't instruct him to shape up or ship out. He doesn't demand Elijah put a smile on his face and He doesn't start giving him some spiritual cheerleading. Instead God leads Elijah on a forty day journey straight to Mount Sinai, the mountain of God.

We aren't told the details of what happened on Elijah's journey. We don't know if he spent most of his time crying his eyes out while walking or even if he had to be pushed and prodded many times along the way. But I think it's pretty important to realize what God did here is He gave Elijah the gift of some time — forty days and forty nights to be exact.

If you've experienced a disappointment in your life, you know that there is nothing like time to give you some much needed perspective. Knowing this I believe that might haven been the intention in the journey that God sent Elijah on. He gave him some time to process, to think, to feel, and ultimately to prepare for meeting the God of Heaven and Earth on that very mountain.

While you and I might not be able to escape the everyday of our lives for forty days and nights, it's important we give ourselves time when we feel despair or disappointment. Maybe it's heading out to a quiet place for an afternoon or weekend. Maybe it's changing your scenery for a day, a week, or a month. Maybe it's turning off the TV and unplugging the internet and reflecting at home. We can all find a place and a few moments in time where we can take the journey that Elijah did.

When we take some time to work through the emotions that accompany "the moment", we're giving ourselves the freedom to heal and, one day, move on. We're allowing our hearts and minds the chance to catch a breath before we have to figure out where we go from here. Ultimately we're allowing more and more perspective to creep in as the minutes tick off the clock.

It's kind of ironic, but that's exactly what I was doing when I wrote this chapter. As I alluded to earlier, in 2005 I underwent what was supposed to be a routine surgery to remove a cyst, but it ended up being anything but routine. One cyst turned into two massive ones that were wrapped around organs and very difficult to remove. What was supposed to be a quick recovery turned into a huge fight for my life when I ended up with a major infection and had to undergo another surgery to re-open the wound to allow it to heal properly. It took six months, but it finally did heal and I thought life would get back to normal afterwards. I was wrong.

The lingering fatigue after the surgeries never really went away and a sleep disorder came along for the ride. There was still a glimmer of hope as I was told that if I underwent treatment for this sleep disorder everything would fall into place. So I filled the next few years with trying one treatment after another in the hopes something would work while nothing seemed to. All the while battling insomnia that was so bad that many nights I couldn't even fall asleep or would only conk out when the sun started to rise, leaving me a zombie to the outside world.

It built to a head over the next few years as I, like mentioned earlier, quit school, cut back on almost everything and underwent a complete lifestyle change to accommodate for this mysterious illness.

Between having to work while I was completely exhausted, being forced to put my plans on hold, and dealing with all the complications that come into your life when you are struggling with an illness, I reached a breaking point. Thankfully I had the opportunity to head to my aunts cottage to spend some time by myself to process all that had happened plus this new suggested diagnosis of Chronic Fatigue Syndrome. A diagnosis that you don't want to face at any age, let alone as someone in their twenties. A diagnosis that in hindsight would look like a walk in the park compared to what was coming down the road, but more on that in later chapters.

So at my aunts cottage, far removed from the distractions of everyday life, I spent a weekend in silence and while the time away didn't change my circumstances, it did shift my perspective. I realized that what's going on in my life isn't the end of the world and that the sun is still going to rise tomorrow. The time away also gave me the moments of silence I needed to have some honest dialogue with God. It was an opportunity to express my disappointment to Him and let Him speak to me. While I still haven't experienced the windstorm, the earthquake, fire, or the gentle whisper that Elijah ended up getting after his forty day journey, I have experienced something altogether different and that is peace. Peace that surpasses all understanding is a very valuable gift.

So don't be afraid to hit the pause button on your life for a few days, weeks or even months if you need to. Give yourself the time to honestly work through what you're feeling and even talk to someone else if you need to. Let time give your eyes a different vision of your circumstances. Things might not change, the picture you had of your future may never reappear, but by taking the journey Elijah did, you will be ready for what comes next — whatever it might be.

CHAPTER TWO

Did I Take a Wrong Turn?

"Comfort and prosperity have never enriched the world as much as adversity has."
— BILLY GRAHAM

With the sleeping problems I've been having, I've been exposed to a lot of late night television. Before my struggles with insomnia, I figured you could only expect to find reruns and infomercials late at night. Imagine my pleasant surprise when I realized late night television was also a hotspot for what was labeled Christian teaching and programming. When I saw those kind of shows on the TV listings, I got excited at the possibility of having the opportunity to use this time late at night to grow deeper in my faith through these programs. Oh, how naive I was.

Now let me insert a little disclaimer: I'm not against Christian television programs, even all those that appear on late night television. There are many Christian TV shows I have been encouraged or blessed by. However, I have noticed that as the lateness of the night increases, so does the amount of prosperity being preached on TV.

One preacher who faithfully came in night after night wanted me to send away for some "miracle manna" that I could eat with the promise it would take away any health or financial problem I might be experiencing. Another teacher wanted to convince me that if my life was anything less than perfect, Satan had a foothold on me and I needed to rebuke him. Another promised that if I sowed a seed of faith into their ministry, aka send them money, God would reward my faithfulness in the form of more money and bigger blessings.

While I was tempted to order the "miracle manna" just to see what it tasted like, I was also tempted to write some of these preachers and ask them some pretty serious questions. For example, were they not familiar with the story of David, the sufferings of Jesus, or perhaps a little book in the Bible called Job?

Many would try to convince us that unless we're wealthy, healthy, and super happy, we've done something wrong or missed some sort of spiritual blessing. I hate to be the one to break it to you, but that's not the way it always works.

We can see this in many stories in the Bible, but a favorite of mine is the story of Joseph (found in Genesis, starting at chapter 37). Here is someone who had it all in the eyes of the world. He was his father's favorite son. He knew through prophetic dreams God had great plans for his life. Regrettably just when everything looked like it was going according to plan, it all changed.

Thanks to his jealous brothers, Joseph was sold into slavery. I know you've probably heard that many times before about Joseph, but just think about what it must have been like. This young man with a bright future was betrayed by the ones who were supposed to love and protect him. He was sent away to another land to live under someone's rule, not knowing a soul and likely not even knowing the language of the land. Isolated and lonely he would have probably started at the bottom of the ranks, doing all of the tasks that the other slaves wouldn't want to do. He would have had to work from early in the morning to late in the evening, never knowing if he would ever be freed from this life or if he would ever even see his family or homeland again.

If that wasn't enough, even though Joseph remained faithful to God throughout his time as a slave, he was still falsely accused of a crime. Offered the chance to sleep with his boss' wife, Joseph does the right thing and refuses. Instead of being rewarded for his integrity, Joseph is accused of rape and sent to jail.

Think of what that would have been like. Sitting in a dark cell in a strange country with no defense lawyer or high powered advocate fighting on your behalf. Knowing without a miracle, you might never again see the light of day again. Having endless hours to ponder about the dreams you had as a young man and the promises you received from God for a bright future.

Now imagine this story took place in the 21st century and someone brought a television into Joseph's cell and he turns it on only to find a TV preacher telling him that he is in that very place since he hasn't given God enough of his money, he hasn't eaten "miracle manna", or he's got the devil inside of him. He changes the channel only to hear that he's a slave turned prisoner because he didn't read the ten steps to spiritual success and if only he would follow step number four, he wouldn't be where he is today.

I know it sounds crazy, but that's the lie being sold to so many of us today. We're told that if life isn't going according to our plan, then we did something to mess it up. As a result, we've got way too many Christians walking around wounded, not knowing how to fix their circumstances when it's not up to them to fix it in the first place.

Am I saying that we never make mistakes or human choices never influence where we end up in life? No. We'll talk about this more in chapter four, but to sum it up for the moment, there are times where we do place ourselves in situations that we shouldn't be in and make bad choices which carry consequences. But my point here is it isn't always the case. Christians go through trials and Christians go through tribulations. It's not because we are big sinners, but because sometimes God allows things to happen to cause us to grow or bring glory to His name. We also need to understand that while we as Christians might be redeemed for eternity in heaven, free from pain and suffering, we still live in a fallen world and do go through difficulties as a result of it (i.e. illness, job loss, family conflict).

If we keep reading the story of Joseph, we find a perfect example of a life story where someone experiences more than one unexpected detour along the way, but still remains faithful. As a result, he is still given amazing opportunities for the future he would have never received had he stayed at home. Namely being appointed to second in command in Egypt — second only to Pharaoh!

What an incredible story of what God did in the life of one of His children who remained faithful even when life didn't go according to plan!

One thing worth noting here is while Joseph ended up in a position that many of us would envy, that position wasn't one he likely was dreaming about when he was a boy growing up at home or even when he was in a prison cell serving time for a crime he didn't commit. Sometimes God changes our direction or we're only clued into the destination once we've arrived. Also at times the destination looks very different than what we had envisioned.

Along with the whole lie of guaranteed prosperity, many of us have a warped view of what being a disciple of Christ really is. Somewhere in the back of our minds we envision that being a disciple comes jobs that are called ministries and immense opportunities such as playing music in front of large audiences in packed-to-the-nose bleed-section arenas or leaving home to minister in a remote area where their definition of good news is hearing that it is going to rain on their crops. While some are called those opportunities, it's not everyone's destination and for good reason. If we were all called to be a traveling musician or missionary, who would be left at your workplace or in your neighborhood to tell them about Jesus?

I'm reminded of a story in the Gospel of Mark. There was a man who might not have lived in a jail cell like Joseph did, but was a prisoner in every other sense of the word. He was demon possessed, to the extent that he was exiled from society and found himself living in a cemetery. In an attempt to control this man, who was clearly out of control, many tried to restrain him with chains and shackles but nothing was strong enough to keep him under control. His life was reduced to wandering throughout the graveyard, yelling at the top of his lungs and hitting himself with stones. That is, until he meets Jesus.

When Jesus stepped into this man's life, He cast out the demons and completely healed him. It wasn't long before word spread throughout the area that the man who once terrorized a town was now perfectly calm and content. Soon a crowd gathered and before long it's time for Jesus to move on to another area. The healed man pleads with Jesus to let him come along. But Jesus had a different idea and instead instructed him,

> *"No, go home to your family, and tell them everything the Lord has done for you and how merciful He has been." (Mark 5:19)*

So what does the man do? According to Mark, he starts to visit nearby towns and tells everyone he comes into contact with about what Jesus did for him and the Bible records that "everyone was amazed by what he told them." (Mark 5:20)

Jesus came into contact with a lot of people, but as we see very clearly with this story, He had a different plan for everyone. Some He brought with Him on His travels, others He instructed to go back their home. Jesus was the same person they were called by, but each one had different callings.

The same goes for you and I. If your calling is looking very different from what you could have ever expected, that doesn't mean it's a bad calling. God didn't suddenly become an umpire who couldn't quite see the ball as it passed the plate and as a result made the wrong call. No, rather it means that the picture God has painted for your future is different from the one you would have painted on the canvas; but that's not a bad thing.

Being a follower of Jesus means that we are willing to follow wherever He leads. While we've attached expectations and conditions to that, the truth is the two words Jesus said in the Gospels were "follow Me." Not to "follow Me and start a worldwide ministry" or "follow Me and all your problems disappear" or "follow Me and you'll get a recording contract" but He simple says "follow Me." Dietrich Bonhoeffer described discipleship in this way,

> *"And what does that text inform us about the content of discipleship? Follow me, run along behind me! That is all. To follow in His steps is something which is void of all content. It gives us no intelligible program for a way of life, no goal or ideal to strive after. It is not a cause which human calculation might deem worth of our devotion, even the devotion of ourselves. What happens? At the call, Levi leaves all that he has — but not simply because he thinks that he might be doing something worthwhile, but simply for the sake of the call. Otherwise, he cannot follow in the footsteps of Jesus."*[1]

Do me a favor and read those last two sentences again. Levi, known to many of us as Matthew, left all he had. It wasn't for some spiritual promotion or dream destiny, but only for the sake of the call.

Are you willing to leave it all behind to follow Jesus for the sake of the call?

The Bible tells us that God has called us by name. He doesn't call us by occupation or by what our future might hold; He calls us by our name.

"Kristen, follow Me."

"_____ (your name here), follow Me."

I'm sure this isn't news to you because chances are if you're reading this book, you're already a follower of Jesus. But what you might not realize is that the same calling you responded to at your salvation is the same calling that you're to be following today. It doesn't matter that your life hasn't turned out as you planned or maybe the plans you thought God was laying out for your life fell through. Those are details, that while they are not insignificant to you, aren't the basis of the call on your life — to follow Him.

"Follow Me."

Those words appear at least 23 times in the New Testament and each time there is no strings attached on our end of the deal. In fact, the only time promises of great things were attached with a call to worship or follow is when Satan was the one doing the calling when he tempted Jesus in the desert. This leads me to believe that if we're making more out of following Jesus than following with no strings attached we aren't hearing the call correctly.

So why is it that we attach conditions in our minds? Why do we believe the lie that if we follow we get a trouble free life filled with big pocketbooks, will win popularity contests and live out a comfortable existence? I don't know where the lie started or why so many of us, myself included, have believed it at one point or another, but I do know this: until we call it for what it is — a lie — we're never going to be content followers of Jesus Christ.

Instead of looking at where we are and rejoicing in where we are at with Jesus and praising Him for what He's given us, we'll keep our eyes on the horizon looking for something more. The danger is that when you are only looking ahead you're bound to miss what is in front of you.

I know that's the case in my own life. Recently I decided that instead of focusing on my plans that weren't working out I was going to praise God for who He is and look instead for opportunities to serve Him where I am. Since that decision, I've had side of the road prayer meetings with strangers. I've had moments where I literally felt like heaven was touching earth while shopping in big box stores. I've had people come up to me and tell me how much they appreciated how I "got them" and the only reason I did understand them is because I have found myself in the same dark place they were. As a result I've had a closer walk with God and the kind of connection with Him that I wouldn't trade for anything. It's amazing what can happen when we don't have the wrong things clouding our perspective, isn't it?

We all need to wake up in the morning and make a daily choice to embrace our call to follow Jesus which is all about surrender and obedience. It is agreeing to live our lives in such a way that is not about glorifying ourselves, but is instead about living our lives in such a way that we shrink away and all that can be seen through us is His glory.

Don't get me wrong. I'm not saying that God won't call you to do something extraordinary during your lifetime; He very well might. The fact that I'm even writing this book proves that case. On the other hand, look at the content of this said book. I would have never been able to write it if I hadn't gone through some extremely hard times and at the time of publishing this, I haven't escaped them. But do you want to know what the amazing thing is? I no longer make it my mission in life to escape my troubles as I've learned that following Jesus doesn't come with an easy street clause. It's kind of like marriage. When two people commit to spend a lifetime together the vows intentionally include "for richer or for poorer, in sickness and in health." What kind of a marriage relationship would it be if the other person got to hit the eject button simply because a storm was blowing in? The best marriages I've witnessed became that kind of deep, enduring love as a direct result of hard times, as hard times is what cemented those two souls together. So why should our lives with Jesus be any different?

We need to get to the place in our hearts where we are following Jesus not because of what He can do for us, but because of who He is and what He's already given. Which, by the way, is far more than any of us could have ever asked for or expected!

Sometimes as believers we can start following because of who He is, but over time lose our focus. We become so wrapped up in church, ministry and life that we hinge our following on what we do rather than on who He is. Maybe that's why we get so disappointed, as discussed in the previous chapter, when the pictures we paint for our lives don't go according to plan.

According to the book of James, plans are something that we as believers should be holding very loosely to,

> *"Look here, you who say, 'Today or tomorrow we are going to a certain town and will stay there a year. We will do business there and make a profit.' How do you know what your life will be like tomorrow? Your life is like the morning fog — it's here a little while, then it's gone. What you ought to say is, 'If the Lord wants us to, we will live and do this or that.' Otherwise you are boasting about your own pretentious plans, and all such boasting is evil." (James 4:13-16)*

At first read that's not an easy truth to swallow, but think about it for a second. Isn't being a disciple of Christ all about our surrender? About giving up our hearts, our lives, our desires, our plans? Where did we ever get the idea that we could follow Christ but still chart the course of our own destiny? Even if we believe God is leading us in a certain direction, we shouldn't hold on so tightly to it that when it doesn't happen, we completely fall apart. After all if we're following Jesus when that door slams shut, then we can know walking through it was never the plan.

Yes it's disappointing, but did you ever stop to consider that that very disappointment could be the plan? Look at the Apostles.

According to history,
> James was beaten, stoned and clubbed to death.
> Andrew and Peter were both crucified.
> John was exiled to an island where he lived alone.
> Paul was beaten, imprisoned, and shipwrecked.

Yet look what God did with their lives!

Sometimes disciple training 101 involves going through some rough times along the way. Sometimes learning to follow in the footsteps of Jesus involves partaking in the suffering of Christ. Often growing in our faith puts us in the path of situations that test us in that very faith.

That doesn't mean we've done something wrong or God is punishing us. No, that's not the case at all. Rather He's allowing us to experience life, real life, in order to let us grow. The writer of James captured it very eloquently:

> *"Dear brothers and sisters, when troubles of any kind come your way, consider it an opportunity for great joy. For you know that when your faith is tested, your endurance has a chance to grow. So let it grow, for when your endurance is fully developed, you will be perfect and complete, needing nothing." (James 1:2-4)*

Think of the time in your life when doors close or the outlook doesn't look ideal as an opportunity to do some spiritual weight training. Maybe you've gone through a trial in the past that helped you lift five faith pounds. Now as a result of the refining you've experienced in your present circumstances you're ready to take on ten pounds. And next time, and oh yes there will be a next time, you can tackle fifteen pounds. Just as the human body needs conditioning to grow in strength, so do we as Christians.

Although the idea of an easy existence is an appealing one, it is not a realistic one. We've been ransomed from our sin, but we're still walking the trenches with everyone else, experiencing less than perfect things in this fallen world that is groaning with us (see Romans 8). But it's in this fallen world that we received a call — a call to follow Christ wherever He leads. It's time to put out of our minds the misconception that this is an easy journey — it's not. Despite that, with Christ as our strength, our peace, and our guide, we're more the conquerors and can walk confidently through each day.

We must continually keep in mind that in the Bible we learn that faithfulness doesn't always equal fruitfulness. Obedience doesn't always mean no obstacles. And trust often takes us down a road with many twists and turns.

CHAPTER THREE

So I'm in the Desert, Now What?

"Wherever you are — be all there."
— JIM ELLIOT

So you're stuck in the middle between where you once were and where you want to be. Life took an unexpected turn and it feels like your life is a phone call that has been stuck on hold for way too long. If that's your journey, you're not alone.

David was also one of these people. For most of his young life, he spent his time in the fields working alone as a lowly shepherd with little recognition. In fact he was so low on the food chain when it came time for Jesse to go meet Samuel with his sons in order for Samuel to proclaim which one of them would be the next King of Israel, David was left at home. Talk about what had to be one big bruise on his ego.

Once David was finally confirmed as God's choice for the next king, he didn't immediately get on the throne. Actually he had many years ahead of him filled with difficult experiences before he finally put on his crown. He worked as an armor bearer, he played his harp for the king, he defeated Goliath, his life was threatened and he was forced to flee and hide in a cave in the middle of no where. He fought battles and wandered like a nomad with no permanent place to call home.

David had the promise of a future as king, but was still forced to live for many years in the in between.

Jesus had a similar story. He had a pretty remarkable story of His birth which attracted much attention, but growing up we're not told that His life looked any differently than the lives of other sons of carpenters. Here is the Son of God and instead of attracting crowds at 16, He was likely putting in long hours, helping Joseph at work. As the Bible tells us, it was only when Jesus was 30 did He start His public ministry.

If it took King David, a man after God's own heart, years of preparation before he was ready for what God had in store for him, who are we to think that we don't need a similar time of waiting? If it took Jesus, the Son of God, nearly 30 years to be prepared for His three and a half years of public ministry, why do we think that we can shortchange our own times of preparation? Instead of trying to speed up our journey from point A to point B, we really need to learn what it means to bloom where we are planted in the in between. As Mother Teresa once said,

> *"I am not called to be successful,*
> *but I am called to be faithful."*

We learn this lesson in the book of Colossians where Paul stated,

> *"And whatever you do or say, do it*
> *as a representative of the Lord Jesus, giving thanks*
> *through him to God the Father." (Colossians 3:17)*

Paul doesn't tell us that we are only a representative of Christ when we're carrying out certain activities that can be labeled as ministry work or are working hard fueling our dreams. He tells us that we are always to be a representative of Jesus, no matter what we are doing. He also instructs us in every situation to be thankful.

In a nutshell that is what blooming where you are planted is all about. Viewing each moment and each task, no matter how mundane, as a chance for you to be shining the light of Christ and being thankful for that very opportunity.

When you learn what it is to bloom where you are planted, it doesn't take long for a feeling of satisfaction to follow. Why? Because when you are blooming where you are planted and are trusting God placed you in that very spot for a reason, you are no longer comparing yourself to others and coming out behind. Instead you are satisfied in knowing this very moment of time is exactly where you are supposed to be, even if you would have never imagined yourself there.

Going back to Joseph, he's a perfect example of this. He probably never in his wildest dreams pictured a future life as a slave. Yet when he was sold into slavery he made a choice to give it his all and in doing so, really bloomed. Instead of being bitter and working to do the minimum to get by, Joseph took his responsibility very seriously and it wasn't long before his boss noticed. After some time, Joseph was placed in charge of all of the other slaves. It didn't change the fact that he was still in the chains of slavery, living in a foreign country, but Joseph made the best of his circumstances and his faithfulness was rewarded.

It was David, the one who was left behind at home by his family, who pointed out,

> *"The Lord gives his own reward*
> *for doing good and for being loyal."*
> *(1 Samuel 26:23)*

Joseph experienced it, both in slavery and then later on in prison. David experienced it, even when he was running from those who wanted to kill him. Jesus experienced it, during his long days and nights of ministry. Their story can become our story too.

The lesson of blooming where you are planted is something that I have been learning a lot about in recent years. Like I mentioned earlier I'm stuck between two places — where I once was and where I want to be. My health problems have evolved over the years from issues defined mostly by poor sleep and fatigue to now experiencing widespread pain and a myriad of strange symptoms. The one thing they have in common is that they hold me back in a significant ways. I can no longer push my body the way I did in my teens and early twenties and if I try, I pay for it for days and weeks to come. It's like my gas tank is empty and all attempts to fill it are in vain. That said, I still do have the same thoughts and ideas and ambitions swirling around in my head, it's just that I don't have enough in me to complete what is in front of me, let alone pursue other endeavors.

It's been a long journey where I've had to learn that productivity is not the key to being fulfilled and my identity doesn't rest in what I do, but rather in who I am. In the process I've learned some pretty interesting things about myself, but it's still been a hard road to walk down.

Even though this isn't chapter I would have written for my life story, I do know that God is still the One holding the pen. He's allowing this to happen and while it's not an ideal time for me, this is still time I've been given and I am responsible for what I do with it. I could sit idly by and let my spiritual growth dry up just as quickly as my goal of a university degree did. While there have been days I've been tempted, I've really been learning what it means to bloom where I'm planted.

At first I couldn't say this, but now I can honestly say that I am content with where I am on this journey. I'm no longer bitter for being asked to walk this road. Instead I can see purpose even in moments of pain. I've come to trust that God has led me into this desert and that He won't leave me here a minute longer than absolutely necessary, and in the meantime, I've been learning to enjoy my time here.

Does that mean I want to stay in this place for the rest of my life? Absolutely not. I am committed to doing what it takes to get well and I work hard at doing everything those on my health team suggest. At the same time though, I'm very much aware that when it comes to these kind of health problems, the ball is not in my court. I can do things to help, but being restored to complete health is in God's hands, not mine. For a reason I can't see from this place He hasn't healed me yet. So in the meantime instead of focusing on what I can't do, I've been making changes in my life to simplify it and invest my energy on what matters. I've learned to say "no" to things that are fleeting and to make time to say "yes" to things that are lasting. I've abandoned climbing the corporate ladder, I've rejected the lie that we are what we own and I've instead embraced making moments with the people I love when I can, instead of waiting for a tomorrow which is not promised to any of us.

Even on days when I have lots of pain or find myself really tired, I've learned to trust God has placed me there for a reason and even low-energy days can be fruitful when it comes to God's kingdom. After all, He doesn't have the same math of success that we do.

At the end of the day what it all comes down to is trust. Without trusting that we follow a God who has a purpose for us and an intention behind every moment, we're never going to arrive at a place where we can truly bloom where we are planted. That is the lesson that our heroes of the faith learned. In Hebrews 11, what has been referred to as the Christian Hall of Faith, the author writes about these heroes,

> *"Each one of these people of faith died not yet having in hand what was promised, but still believing."*[2]

Go back and read that verse again. Each one of those heroes went to the grave not having in hand what was promised to them, yet they still believed in their God from start to finish. That's faith. That's trust. And that's what growing in a desert and blooming where we are planted, is all about. It's taking the moment with trust in the One who created it and living it out for His kingdom. I believe Erich Fromm got a head start on unintentional translation of this verse when he wrote,

> *"To hope means to be ready at every moment for that which is not yet born, and yet not become desperate if there is no birth in our lifetime."*[3]

So how do we arrive at this kind of hope and trust? Is it out there to be found? Should we be looking for it? Or is it just going to magically come to us one day? This may not be a popular idea to talk about, but truthfully, I don't think there is a formula. Arriving at the destination of trust can present a slightly different journey for each of us.

For me a big part of solidifying my trust in God was realizing just how big He is in comparison to how small I am. I can admit it; I'm a complete and utter mess. There are days when I can't figure out the difference between where I am going and where I am coming from. I have trouble keeping track of appointments; without the calendar on my computer, I'd probably never show up for anything. It's taken many mistakes to realize I was on the wrong road in life, headed for the wrong destination. If we followed a God who would say "I told you so" to someone, I would have heard it many times over by now.

Yet in the midst of this mess, I know that not only does God love me, but He directs my path. He is someone who I can follow with confidence. Why? Let's just listen to what has been said on good authority about Him,

> *"God's breath sends the ice, freezing wide expanses of water. He loads the clouds with moisture, and they flash with His lighting." (Job 37:10-11)*

> "God looks down from heaven on the entire human race." (Psalm 53:2a)

> "For by His great power He rules forever. He watches every movement of the nations; let no rebel rise in defiance... Our lives are in His hands and He keeps our feet from stumbling." (Psalm 66:7,9)

> "Heaven is my throne and the earth is my footstool." (Isaiah 66:1)

> "I know men and I tell you that Jesus Christ is no mere man. Between Him and every other person in the world there is no possible term of comparison. Alexander, Caesar, Charlemagne, and I have founded empires. But on what did we rest the creation of our genius? Upon force. Jesus Christ founded His empire upon love; and at this hour millions of men would die for Him." (Napoleon)

God is all-powerful, all-knowing, and all-worthy of our trust. This is a lesson that Job learned well. After experiencing the tremendous loss of his family, his health, even his wealth, Job had a lot of questions for God and was unsure as to what His plan was. In fact, the book of Job is filled with over thirty chapters of questions for God and observations from Job's friends of why this might be happening to him.

What's interesting to me is that when God speaks up in His three chapter monologue for Job, He doesn't offer answers. Instead He only presents Job with more questions, such as: "Have you ever commanded the morning to appear and cause the dawn to rise in the East?" and "Have you ever visited the treasuries of snow? Have you seen where hail is made and stored?"

God doesn't try to explain to Job why. Instead He makes Job aware of the vast difference that exists between all of us and our Creator. Where God is big, we are small. Where God is all-knowing, we have limited understanding. That said, even if God tried to explain it, Job in his humanness would not be able to comprehend it. Which is why God doesn't ask us to understand, He does asks us to trust.

Read Job 38-42 and ask yourself if your life is better placed in His hands or yours? Ask yourself if a God like that is worth trusting. Hopefully we will all arrive at the same conclusion that the writer of Proverbs did,

> *"A person's steps are directed by the Lord.*
> *How then can anyone understand their own way?"*
> *(Proverbs 20:24, NIV)*

When we trust in the God who directs our steps, something amazing happens. We no longer bear the weight of trying to orchestrate all of our outcomes. As a result suddenly the load gets lighter, the sky looks brighter, and our step has just a bit more bounce to it. When we are walking in confidence, trusting the God who is leading us, life can be a pretty amazing adventure.

CHAPTER FOUR

When We Can't Drive in Reverse

"There will come a time when you think everything is finished. That will be the beginning."
— LOUIS L'AMOUR

There are times in our lives when we will face a closed door because we did the one thing many of us fear the most: we made a mistake.

Maybe for you the mistake was taking a job you knew wasn't God's best for you. Maybe the mistake was entering into a relationship you shouldn't have. Maybe it was not walking through a door God had opened. Maybe it was disobeying Him by sinning. Or maybe the mistake was as common as not consulting God in the first place.

Our mistakes take on different shapes and faces, but they all have the potential to be accompanied by damaging consequences which can take us off the road that we started on.

That was the story of Jenna. In high school Jenna had fantastic marks, an active social life, and knew exactly where she wanted to go in life. She loved the Lord and wanted nothing more than to follow Him. But one decision changed it all for Jenna. She started dating a guy who she knew was not a believer and did not hold the same values, but at the time she didn't care since the relationship seemed fun and convenient. It wasn't long before Jenna was pregnant.

Suddenly dreams of college were replaced with the worries of raising a child. Her hopes of marrying a Godly man who loved Jesus completely and would lead her family in God's ways were replaced by the reality of the man she was with and the many ways he didn't measure up as a believer or a father. All her hopes, aspirations, and dreams went up in smoke. It was not because having a child is a bad thing, a child is one of the biggest blessings a person can receive. It was because she went against God's plan to arrive there.

While Jenna knows and has experienced the forgiveness and grace of God, she still is stuck in a rut, with the father of her child having long since abandoned her and her baby. My heart breaks for Jenna, not only for the pain she carries now, but for those lonely nights when the only thing that crosses her mind is what could have been.

Truthfully the mistakes we make can completely change our course in life. But that isn't the greatest tragedy. The greatest tragedy is when one mistake turns into a lifetime of them. Sadly, this is a common occurrence.

Too often the shame of our mistakes propels us to try and dig our way out, or at least make things look better on the surface. In the process we make one mistake and instead of repenting, turn the one mistake into two and two into three and thus the story continues.

That was King David's story. After years of waiting to take on his God-given mission, David was finally crowned King of Israel. Years on the run were traded in for title of ruler and the address of a palace. Yet while David was once a mighty warrior for whatever reason, on this one occasion we know of, he decided to stay at home while his army was off fighting a fierce battle. As a result David was about to learn a lesson: it's a dangerous thing to have too much time on our hands.

After wandering around the palace, he found himself on the roof. While taking in the sights of his kingdom, off in the distance David saw a beautiful woman, Bathsheba, taking a bath. David liked what he saw and instead of looking away, lusted after her. This was mistake number one. Unfortunately the story doesn't end there.

David put his lust into motion when he sent someone to find out who she was. Even after finding out she was married to another man, he still sent for her and ended up sleeping with her. That was mistake number two and three, but again the story doesn't end there.

Later Bathsheba sends word to David that she is pregnant. Instead of taking responsibility for his sin, David selfishly decides the best course of action is to cover up what he's done. So he calls Bathsheba's husband Uriah home from war and does everything he can to ensure Uriah spends the night with his wife. His plan backfires when Uriah honorably refuses to go home to his wife saying,

> *"The Ark and the armies of Israel and Judah are living in tents, and Joab and my master's men are camping in the open fields. How could I go home to wine and dine and sleep with my wife? I swear that I would never do such a thing." (2 Samuel 11:11)*

Rather than being convicted and humbled by the actions of a righteous man, David is still desperately caught up in a quest to cover up his sin. Instead of stopping at adultery, David resorts to murder.

He sends Uriah back into battle and instructs the head of his army to put Uriah into the fiercest part of the battle and then pull back, knowing full well that Uriah will die at the hands of the enemy. Joab follows David's instructions and Uriah is killed. The story continues,

> "When Bathsheba heard that her husband was dead, she mourned for him. When the period of mourning was over, David sent for her and brought her to the palace, and she became one of his wives. Then she gave birth to a son. But the Lord was very displeased with what David had done."
> (2 Samuel 11:26-27)

You see in David's master plan, he neglected to take into consideration one fact when orchestrating such an elaborate cover-up: God was watching. The same God who showed His favor to David in the past and who granted him a place on the throne is the same God who laid down laws against adultery, deceit, and the taking of another man's life. To the world around him, David might have appeared pure and even noble for taking care of Uriah's wife after he died, but God could see the bigger picture. He saw David's sins and He saw how David refused to take responsibility for them.

While it's very easy for us to point our fingers in David's direction and call him a fool for ducking responsibility with this crazy cover-up, how often do you and I do the same thing? Maybe we haven't gone as far as murder to avoid the shame of our sin, but we all have sinned trying to cover up a mistake.

There is child who breaks the rules, doesn't accept the consequences, lies and points the finger at anyone but himself.

There is the person who crashes their car into one that's parked and leaves the scene of the accident to avoid facing the consequences, all the while breaking the law in the process.

There is the husband or wife who has an affair. Instead of admitting and repenting after mistake, they trade in their family for this new relationship. Only to wake up one day and realize this new life wasn't what it was cracked up to be and they can see a wake of pain left in their absence.

We've all made wrong choices after making a mistake and those secondary choices can often do more damage than the first mistake did.

So how do we avoid making mistake number two and three after mistake number one? It only happens when we accept responsibility for what we've done.

This isn't easy to do because we live in a society that is nearly obsessed with avoiding responsibility. Just recall a recent scandal in the news. Chances are whether it involved a politician or a celebrity, the scandal held fast to the theme of "it wasn't my fault." This is so common it's become a cultural phenomenon. As Joan McGregor, a philosopher at Arizona State University, pointed out,

> *"Responsibility is waning. The strong sense of holding people responsible is getting more and more difficult. We still hold people responsible all the time in a legal sense. But in a moral sense, it's as though no one is responsible anymore."*[4]

Rather than taking responsibility many of us are caught up in something even worse — the blame game.

The blame game is one with no rules other than to cast blame on someone else and it's something we do all the time. We retort, "It's not me. It's MTV or my parents or my circumstances or my boss or my financial situation." The list of excuses goes on and on and on.

Maybe you're reading this and thinking you're not like that. You're absolutely certain you own up for what you do wrong in your life. Maybe you do, but maybe you don't and are just so used to doing it that you can't see the difference any more. Here's a little test to find out. Read this list of statements and ask yourself for each one have you ever found yourself saying it?

I was late, because of traffic.

I'm not being paid enough, so I...

If my parents hadn't..., I wouldn't...
I'm so busy that I don't have time to eat right or exercise.
I'm sorry, but...
I don't have enough money because...
I would have had a better mark, but I...
If it wasn't for that person, I wouldn't have...
You gave me no choice but to...
If only I had a different boss, I would do better at work.
I'm not growing because the pastor's sermons aren't deep enough.
I wouldn't have done that but....

The list of possible blame statements could go on and on. I could even write another book if I was so inclined and call it "Blame Statements 101."

The point of this exercise is to open our minds to the possibility that we too could be caught up in the cycle of blaming other people or circumstances when really the problem lies with us.

Which is exactly what we see go down in the Garden of Eden. Adam and Eve both heard God's warnings about not eating the fruit. But my, it must have looked tasty and soon resisting the forbidden was something they no longer wanted to do. Eve had some first, then Adam took the plunge. But when God confronted them about it, they both tried to cast the blame for their actions on someone else. As author David Zimmerman noted,

> *"Adam and Eve each denied their own responsibility when confronted by God because they saw themselves as too important to be wrong, to be weak, to vulnerable to the shrewdness of a mere serpent...*
> *We're too important for silly rules. We can't be expected to keep promises we made after circumstances change. Give us enough time, and we'll figure out who's really to blame for the trouble we find ourselves in."*[5]

This presents a huge problem as when we deny responsibility for our actions, we don't leave much room for change. By blaming someone else for our shortcomings we are really saying we have no control over our behavior and given the same set of circumstances, the same thing is going to happen. This kind of attitude sets us up to fall and fall again.

They left the money out, so who could blame me for taking it?

She dressed seductively, so where else were my thoughts supposed to go?

Everyone drives fast, so if I don't I'm setting myself up to get in an accident when they pass me.

If he hadn't made me so mad, I would have never hit him.

If we try hard enough, we can come up with an excuse for anything. While this might help us feel self-justified for a moment, it's a dangerous way of thinking as it sets us up to constantly repeat the same mistake over and over again. Instead of falling, repenting, and moving on, we get trapped in an endless cycle. Trip, fall, wasn't my fault, trip, fall, wasn't my fault, trip, fall, wasn't my fault. Can anything good ever come out of that way of living?

If you have found yourself facing closed doors or unexpected circumstances because of a choice of your own making the best thing you can do for yourself is stop making excuses and own up to what you did. Then do a complete 180 and walk in the other direction, leaving those sins and mistakes behind. That's humility, that's repentance, and that's something that God requires of all of His children,

> *"So humble yourselves before God. Resist the devil, and he will flee from you. Come close to God, and God will come close to you. Wash your hands, you sinners; purify your hearts for your loyalty is divided between God and the world. Let there be tears for what you have done. Let there be sorrow and deep grief. Let there be sadness*

> *instead of laughter, and gloom instead of joy. Humble yourselves before the Lord, and He will lift you up in honor."* (James 4:7-10)

When we humble ourselves in this way, coming to God on our knees, God honors that. Yes, in admitting we messed up and taking account for our sins we might have our own rock bottom moment, but the beauty about hitting rock bottom is there is no where to go but up.

Just ask anyone who has ever gone through an addiction program like Alcoholics Anonymous or something similar. One of the reasons these programs are very effective is because the first few steps involve recognition, responsibility and removing denial. Saying "I'm [name] and I'm an alcoholic" is an extremely powerful statement and I'm sure it's the starting point to healing for many because it removes everyone else out of the equation. It's a short, simple statement that recognizes the problem and doesn't make room for excuses for it. It's one of those "this is it" statements.

I think we would all do well to come up with our own "this is it" statement.

I'm Kristen and I picked the wrong degree.

I'm Matthew and I didn't walk into the door God had opened.

I'm Lauren and I purposely hurt someone I love, then blamed it on them.

I'm Shawn and I choose financial security over taking a step of faith.

I'm Riley and my selfishness is hurting my family.

Could you imagine the healing that could take place in our lives if we gave ourselves permission to do this? Taking off the mask, getting out in the open with our issues, admitting to ourselves, our friends, and most importantly, our God, that we made a mistake.

When we realize we messed up and openly confess to God,

we're giving Him something to work with. God is in the redemption business, but how can He redeem someone who thinks they are perfect and are in no need of redemption? It just doesn't seem to work that way. The story of redemption throughout the Bible shares a similar pattern: believe, repent, then He redeems.

We see that as God takes Saul, the very man who persecuted and killed believers, and turns him into Paul, the greatest evangelist of his time.

We see that as God takes Peter, the same man who denied Christ three times and uses him to start the early church.

We see that as God takes David, a man whose mistakes were plenty and uses him to lead God's chosen nation and turns his family into a dynasty.

We see that as God takes John Mark, who deserted Paul and Barnabas during their first missionary journey and gracefully allows him back into the ministry.

That's the story of grace, the Gospel of not just forgiveness, but also of redemption. God uses the weak, the ones who have failed and the ones who had run out of second chances long ago.

I find it to be encouraging considering I have made mistakes. But in these stories I learn that even one or two mistakes doesn't stop the love of God from forgiving me or the grace of God from redeeming me. I might start down the wrong path, but God through His correction and guidance is able to get me to where I need to go.

The story of the Gospel is through His wounds we are healed. We are healed from the damage sin made on our eternal souls, healed from the bondage that wraps us in its grasp and healed from the regrets and mistakes of the past. The Bible tells us very clearly that it doesn't matter where we've been or what we've done, when we turn to Him, God welcomes us back with open arms.

Some Christians believe God's welcoming grace only applies to those who didn't know Christ before they messed up, but I believe the opposite is true. If we look at the story of the prodigal son, we see that the relationship severed was between father and child — the same sort of relationship we enter into with God after accepting Christ.

Grace doesn't stop being extended to us after we've said the sinner's prayer — that is only just the beginning! Grace is a continual gift which allows us not only to be forgiven for past wrongs, but gives us the opportunity to be trusted again for service. Although it doesn't mean we should purposely act irresponsibly or squander what we've been given; it does take a huge weight off of our shoulders when we do mess up.

And we will mess up. We will hold on when we should have let go. We will walk away when we should have run. We will go when we should have stayed and we will hurt others when we should have loved. But God forgives, He forgets, and best of all, He restores.

As Brennen Manning wrote in his amazing book, Abba's Child,

> *"God not only forgives and forgets our shameful deeds but even turns their darkness into light."*[6]

So what about you? You may have made a big mistake that derailed you from the tracks, but are you going to let one mistake be the defining point for the rest of your life? Or are you going to pick yourself up, accept responsibility for your choices and humbly ask God for forgiveness?

Then and only then, will you see a beautiful thing happen. The same God who sent the beauty of a rainbow after the destructive force of a flood is going to come into your life and do some of His best redemption work. Maybe He'll place your feet upon a new path. Maybe He'll completely put back together what you thought had permanently fallen apart. Maybe He'll use your story to touch the hearts and lives of others. Or maybe He's got something else in store for you completely — it doesn't matter.

What does matter is we follow a God who does some of His best work in the greatest messes that mankind has been known to make. Nothing or no one is beyond the repair of the Master Carpenter. It's time to wake up and be excited for the great creation He's building with our lives.

Redemption is more than just a word. It's the story that God is writing in all of our lives.

CHAPTER FIVE

Throw It to See If It'll Stick

> *"If you're so fearful of failure that you never set up your row of tin cans to shoot at, you're not very likely to hit any at all. Failure is not the end. For the person who determines to learn from it, failure is a friend."*
> — RALPH F. WILSON

I can remember when I was younger I would watch in awe as my Mom would cook spaghetti in the kitchen. My favorite part was when the noodles were done boiling because she'd take one noodle out of the pot and throw it up against the wall. If it stuck she knew the noodles were ready. If not, she'd let the noodles continue to boil.

As a child this process was fascinating for two reasons. First of all, it wasn't often my Mom would go around throwing food on the wall (generally that was discouraged in our household). Secondly, it was an example of how something so simple like spaghetti sticking to a wall could tell you so much.

Today I find the whole idea of throwing spaghetti up against a wall fascinating for a completely different reason. It's mainly due to the reality that my life has become it's own little version of "throw it to see if it'll stick." Stay with me for a minute. It's like I've got this bowl of opportunities and of things I worked so hard for and dreamed so long about. Yet all I can do is keep throwing these items out of the bowl in any direction I can think of to see if it'll stick somewhere, anywhere.

One example of this is my education. For many years I worked so hard on completing my university degree by correspondence. It was something I loved doing and had pushed through a lot of obstacles to do. But then there I was, a little over a year away from being done and my health took a nose dive, closing the door for me to continue on. I was left with nothing else but to throw those courses out to see if they would stick somewhere.

Then there's this book. I spent a lot of time working on the manuscript not knowing if it would stick anywhere when I was finished. At the time of writing this chapter, nothing has stuck. I've got no publishing deal, no golden opportunity. All I have is a message I really believe in and would love to see spread to the masses.

I know I'm not alone in this "throw it to see if it'll stick" phase of life. I'm accompanied by the person desperate for a job who is putting out application after application, hoping for something, anything.

I'm traveling next to the musician who believes in their music and believes God has called them to go further on, but they're seeing no doors opening.

I'm sharing the roadway with the widow who had made a lifetime of plans with their spouse, but are now left to pick up the pieces of their shattered dreams alone.

We all have our stories. We all have our different versions of the noodles we throw up against the wall to see if they'll stick, but in the end this process can be a very dangerous one when it comes to our future. Why? Because all too often people stop trying after they've seen a door slammed shut one too many times.

Let's go back to the example of my Mom throwing noodles up against the wall. Let's say she'd been cooking those noodles for 5 minutes over the time the box said and still they wouldn't stick. She keeps throwing until six minutes past, then eight, and then ten. How long do you think she would keep throwing the noodles against the wall before giving up?

Frequently we throw items out there to see if they will stick somewhere, anywhere. When we try and try and try again and they don't stick we start to get discouraged. That very discouragement can lead to quitting if we're disappointed enough times. It can also lead to quitting because for many of us our fear of failure is stronger than our desire to succeed.

Don't believe me? Look around in your own life long enough and I'm sure you can come up with more than one example of a situation where you may have quit prematurely as you were afraid of failing. Maybe you dropped out of a course rather than receive a failing grade. Maybe you dumped your boyfriend or girlfriend out of a fear you didn't have what it takes to make a relationship work or because you were convinced that they were going to break up with you. Or maybe you stayed stuck in a rut in your job because you were scared of the rejection that comes with sending out application after application. All of these things have one very big thing in common: they all trace back to our fear of failure.

Having a fear of failure is such a popular phobia it's even been given it's own name: Atychiphobia. Have you ever had an atychiphobic moment? I know I've had my fair share. They often come when we least expect them. They are very good at disguising themselves as other things (i.e. "the Lord wasn't leading me"), and they can stop us in our tracks like nothing else can.

I'm convinced atychiphobia has become one of the biggest crises we are facing here in North America. As our pride continues to build, our atychiphobia continues to build as well. Why? On the premise hat the two are directly correlated. If we weren't so hung up on what other people thought of us (pride), would we really be so afraid to fail? The one hinges on the other and unfortunately as a society our pride only continues to grow.

This phenomenon is leaving a wake of consequences in its path as when people fear failure, they also stunt the growth of their success — not only in the Kingdom of God, but even in our worldly dealings.

Think about the things we hold oh so dearly.

Would Steve Jobs have given us the iPhone, iPod, and iTunes had he been afraid of failure?

Would Bono have ever gotten behind a microphone if he was paralyzed by the thought of failing?

Would Mark Zuckerberg have ever invited his friends onto a little website he created called Facebook if he was terrified the whole thing was going to be a flop?

All of these people stood up in the face of tremendous odds and had the guts to go forward with an idea they believed in. As a result the world as we know it was turned upside down.

Even speaking in the Christian world, most of the heroes of the faith we hold in such high regard had failed before. What set them apart though was not only that they had failed before, but they had a willingness to not let their fear of failing paralyze them.

Abraham was one of these people. During a drought instead of trusting God to provide the life-giving water that was needed, he fled to Egypt. But we remember him as the Father of the nation of Israel, not as a sprinter from trouble.

Barnabas is remembered as being a great encourager. He was even referred to as an apostle although he was not one of the original twelve. Yet he had to be corrected by Paul for not doing the right thing by avoiding the Gentile believers.

Moses led the people of Israel to the Promised Land, right through the Red Sea, but when it came time to enter he was stopped by the shores because of his disobedience to God.

Solomon allowed his wives to lead him off the path. He went against the plan by allowing marriage amongst foreigners (a big no-no in those days), and even drafted the people into Israel into labor in order to build God's temple (another bad idea). But do we remember Solomon for any of these things? No. We remember him for his wise words and life instructions.

And then there's Peter. If there was a club for failure, Peter might have been called the President. For as many high moments he had, he also had moments I'm sure he wished he could have taken back. From denying Jesus three times to cutting off a guy's ear in haste to telling Jesus that he wouldn't suffer (and thus being renounced by Christ), Peter had his moments of mess-ups. Yet this is the same man who was an essential force in the spreading of Christ's message and is often referred to as one of the founders of the early church.

With these people though it's important to note it's not their failure that we remember them by. It's their successes. Get a group of people together and ask them to say a phrase or word to associate with each one of these people mentioned and chances are the list would look somewhat like this:

Abraham — Father of Israel

Barnabas — Encourager

Moses — Red Sea Crossing

Solomon — Wisdom & the construction of God's temple

Peter — Founder of the early church

Their story can be yours and mine too. If we allow ourselves to get past our mistakes and we let ourselves step over our fear of failure, then the past doesn't have to be the end of our stories.

It was Theodore Roosevelt who once said,

> *"The only man who never makes a mistake is the man who never does anything."*

We as believers can be tricked into thinking that by doing nothing we're actually doing God a service since we're avoiding the chance of failure. That's a lie Satan wants us to believe because if he could get every Christian to believe it, no one would ever get anything done in the Kingdom of God.

The truth of the matter is, the only way we are going to get over our fear of failure is to embrace the idea that it's okay to fail.

After all, what is failure?

Is it the end of our lives?

The end of our worlds?

Or maybe, just maybe, is it an opportunity to learn something from our experiences?

That's what Thomas Edison believed. This is a man who tried many different formulas and inventions and practices and in the process, came up with more wrong answers than he did right ones. Yet Edison kept pressing on, even when the walls came crashing down around him.

The story is told that when Edison was 67 years old his building caught on fire and although fire companies from all over came to try and put it out, the fire took its hold and everything was destroyed. While the fire did over two million dollars in damage, Edison was only insured for a small portion of it and besides losing all of his work, he was left facing a major shortfall. Yet the morning after the fire, what did Edison do? He looked at the ruins and declared,

> *"There is great value in disaster. All our mistakes are burned up. Thank God we can start anew."*[7]

Three weeks after the fire Thomas Edison constructed the first phonograph.

Where many of us would have only seen the flames, Edison saw an opportunity for a fresh start. He took that opportunity and instead of fearing more failure or disaster or calamity, he kept pressing on.

Imagine what our world would look like today if every person who failed or faced a roadblock just gave up? They stopped trying? They stopped throwing stuff against the wall to see if it would stick? The world would certainly be a much different place.

In our lives not every swing will produce a home run, but it's okay. It's in giving ourselves permission to fail true freedom comes.

Freedom to be who we are without worrying about letting other people down. Freedom to take a step of faith without being paralyzed by the possibility of looking foolish. Freedom to walk where God leads without looking around for approval before we take the first step.

To the outside world our path isn't going to make sense. It probably won't even make sense to us, but it's not the point. The point is we haven't let failure push us off the path to where we believe God is leading. We may look foolish, but it's not like we haven't been forewarned. In his letter to the church in Corinth Paul writes,

> *"Since God in His wisdom saw to it that the world would never find him through human wisdom, He has used our foolish preaching to save all who believe."* (1 Corinthians 1:21)

In the Kingdom of God, everything is turned upside down in comparison to the world's way of doing things. The first shall be last. The last will be first. The wise are fools. And the fools are the ones we should be listening to.

It's reverse logic, but in embracing this logic and understanding that Christianity means checking our pride at the door, we can move forward to the destination God has in mind for us. A destination we would have never arrived at if we were caught up in being scared to fail or afraid to look foolish.

That's the story of our heroes of the faith. Not that they never feared or never failed, but that their faith in God outweighed their fears or failures.

Peter was afraid to get out of the boat, but he had more faith than fear and was able to walk on water.

Jacob was afraid to meet Esau, but he had more faith than fear and was able to reunite with his brother.

Nehemiah was afraid to approach the king, but he had more faith than fear and was allowed to rebuild Jerusalem.

Esther was also afraid to approach the king, but she had more faith than fear and the Jewish people were saved.

On the other hand, the Israelites saw the powerful people living in the Promised Land and their fear outweighed their trust in God. As a result they wandered in the desert for forty years.

Jonah was afraid to preach to the people of Nineveh and had more fear than faith. Consequently he spent some time in a whale's stomach.

What it all comes down to is not do we fear, but does your fear outweigh your faith and trust in God? God wants us to trust Him with every fiber of our being,

> *"This is my command — be strong and courageous! Do not be afraid or discouraged. For the Lord your God is with you wherever you go." (Joshua 1:9)*

> *"For God has not given us a spirit of fear and timidity, but of power, love, and self-discipline." (2 Timothy 1:7)*

By conquering our fear we aren't guaranteed the road is going to go exactly the way we want it to; however we can walk in confidence by knowing that we aren't being held back by our fears or insecurities.

This period in our lives of throwing stuff out to see if it'll stick can be frustrating when on the surface we don't seem to be making progress. But we need to hang onto a really important truth: just like noodles only stick to the wall when they are ready to eat, God will only let things in our lives stick when those things are ready to go forth.

In my case it unfolded in a beautiful way that I couldn't see at the time. Remember those courses I mentioned from university? I don't believe it's any coincidence they were mostly in business. In 2012 when my health had improved to the point where I could add more to my plate, it wasn't finishing my education I felt God calling me to; it was opening a business. Today Jumpstart Media is up and running! No mistake that those very courses I never thought I'd be able to use were essential in giving me the knowledge I needed to open the business and get it on a good path. Only God could have seen that far down the road; I certainly couldn't have.

So today we keep throwing things against the wall to see if they will stick, but instead of shaking our heads in frustration as they fall, we'll trust. And when the day does come when one of those things stick, we'll rejoice in knowing it's happening in the right time, in the right season, for the right reason.

CHAPTER SIX

Ideal Destination or Idol?

"Why do we cling to what we lose while we ignore what we still hold?"
— DUIKER THE HISTORIAN

Not long after becoming a Christian I decided reading through the Bible would be a great idea. I got one of those one year Bible reading plans and jumped into Genesis.

While reading the Old Testament my first time from cover to cover, I couldn't help but have the response of just shaking my head after reading many of the stories. I couldn't understand the nation of Israel or the way they they would act in many instances.

I mean, here they are, God's chosen nation. Out of all the nations and tongues and tribes, He calls them His own. He paves the way for them to escape the chains of slavery in Egypt and start their own nation in the Promised Land.

He leads them through one miracle after another, from a Red Sea parting to the miraculous appearance of manna every morning. He guards them, protects them and loves them. When it comes to asking for something in return, His list of expectations are pretty short. One is in Exodus,

> *"I am the LORD your God... You must not have any other gods but me." (Exodus 20:2-3)*

Sounds pretty simple, right? They are following the same God who led them out of Egypt and after seeing the incredible displays of His power and might, who else would they want to turn to?

As it turns out it's a pretty long list. A few examples being,

A golden calf that they built with their own two hands (Exodus 32);

Astarte, the goddess of the Zidonians (1 Kings 11:5);

Baal, the supreme male god that complemented Astarte (Numbers 22:42);

Chemosh, the god of Moab and of Ammon (1 Kings 11:7, Judges 11:24);

Dagon, the god that the Philistines worshiped who they believed was partly man and partly fish (1 Samuel 5:2). Maybe that's where Hans Christian Anderson got his inspiration from;

Molech, represented by a statue with its arms stretched out, ready to receive the children that were to be sacrificed to this god (Leviticus 18:21);

It seems as though every time the Israelites came into contact with a new culture, they embraced the foreign gods as a part of their own religion. All after seeing with their own eyes the Lord defeat their enemies; after tasting with their own mouths the manna that came down from heaven; and after feeling with their own toes the dry floor of the Red Sea beneath their feet.

It didn't matter how much God did for them or how often He displayed His power, it wasn't enough to capture their attention or their whole-hearted worship.

While I have caught myself shaking my head at this many times, I also can see myself so very clearly in their story. My idol might not be called Dagon or I might have never carved something to bow to out of wood, but I bow down just the same.

To my bank account.
To my education.
To my possessions.
To my plans.
Even to myself.

As we learn first from Jesus and then again from the Apostle Paul, idolatry isn't limited to worshipping foreign gods or items created with human hands. It involves anything which takes the place that should be occupied by God in our lives,

> *"No one can serve two masters. For you will hate one and love the other, or be devoted to one and despise the other." (Luke 16:13)*

> *"You must worship the Lord your God and serve only Him." (Matthew 4:10)*

> *"So put to death the sinful, earthly things lurking within you. Have nothing to do with sexual immorality, impurity, lust and evil desires. Don't be greedy, for a greedy person is an idolater, worshipping the things of this world." (Colossians 3:5)*

This is an important lesson to learn, especially on our journey towards some ideal destination which occupies our minds. Why? Because it's very easy to turn even something good into an idol, even something so innocent looking as our dreams for the future.

As John Calvin once wrote,

> *"The evil in our desire typically does not lie in what we want, but in what we want too much."*

While there is nothing wrong with wanting life to turn out one way or another, it does become a problem when we want that destination more than anything or when the idea of facing a closed door seems like the absolute worst thing that could happen. In these situations we have to ask ourselves, is our idea of the future something we hold as ideal? Or has it become more than that? Has it become something we bow to as an idol?

How can you know for sure? Well, Jesus gives us a pretty good test to find out just how highly we're holding up anything in our lives. If we flip over to Luke 12, we find ourselves interrupting the story just after Jesus had finished describing all of the things God has provided for us, including eternal life. Then He springs this profound statement,

> *"Wherever your treasure is, there the desires of your heart will also be." (Luke 12:34)*

By flipping around this statement we can find out if our dream destination has become an idol. How? By asking ourselves an honest question which is not "where is my treasure?" Sadly many of us would probably respond with the answer "God" to this question and we'd be stretching the truth. The real test question is to ask, "what are the ultimate desires of my heart?"

Are our deepest desires,
Getting ahead?
Building a ministry?
Moving onto a new job?
Getting married?
Being financially secure?

If the answer to any one of those questions is "yes", you might just be holding your future up a little too highly and thus creating your own idol out of it.

Again, it's not the dream or destination itself which is wrong; it's what we're doing with it that is.

The truth is God wants to have the number one spot in our lives, both in who we worship and in what we desire — not number two and certainly not number ten. He wants to be considered Supreme and Lord above all else. And that's His rightful place; He's earned that spot on the throne,

> "I am the Lord; that is my name! I will not give my glory to anyone else, nor share my praise with carved idols." (Isaiah 42:8)

But all too often in life we cast Him off the throne and replace Him with other things. When our ideals become our idols we start playing a very dangerous game of Russian Roulette in our lives. While sometimes the chamber of the gun is empty when we fire, other times it isn't and the fallout is not pretty.

That's the story of the young woman who made an idol out of getting married and having a family. The idol was so big in her life she couldn't recognize that the relationship she saw as God's gift to her was actually a trap she easily fell into.

That's the story of the family who got so committed to the idea of missions they forgot who the mission should be all about. Instead they started bowing to the programs and the plans, ignoring the opportunities to serve the people God has placed right in front of them.

That's the story of the man who made an idol out of a certain promotion at work. The promotion came and went without his name anywhere on the list. Now he's devastated and too paralyzed to see God's best is just around the corner.

Idols blind us to the blessings that God has placed in front of us and they turn us into people who stumble around in the darkness, making one poor choice after another. The truth is, by placing our trust and hope in anything other than God, we're living a very foolish existence,

> *"The person who made the idol never stops to reflect, 'Why, it's just a block of wood! I burned half of it for heat and used it to bake my bread and roast my meat. How can the rest of it be a god? Should I bow down to worship a chunk of wood?' The poor deluded fool feeds on ashes. He trusts something that can't help him at all. Yet he cannot bring himself to ask, 'Is this idol that I'm holding in my hand a lie?'" (Isaiah 44:19-20)*

Those are very powerful words, spoken to a nation who had constructed many idols and bowed to many gods other than the Lord. They are also very powerful words for our society, which has made a hobby out of bowing to any idol we can find that might fill the voids which flood our souls.

We as Christians need to be evaluating our lives for idols and commit to getting rid of them as soon as they are recognized. As not only do they remove God from the throne in our lives, but they also change us. As Thomas Merton pointed out so wisely,

> *"A life is either spiritual or not spiritual at all. No man can serve two masters. Your life is shaped by the end you live for. You are made in the image of what you desire."*

We are a reflection of who or what we worship. If your idol is money, it's not going to be long before your life reeks of greed. If your idol is a degree, it's not going to be long before you start smelling of supremacy. If your idol is recognition, you're going to be so twisted by insecurities that any ovation you get will never be enough.

On the other hand if God is sitting on the throne of our lives, it's not going to be long before we start reflecting His nature and His goodness. Along the way we'll also experience His peace, His love, His strength, His mercy.

When we put God first, everything else falls into its rightful place. Our dreams, goals, and desires will either continue to catch fire as we grow closer to Him or if that's not what He'd have for us, they'll fall away. If we keep our eyes focused on Him, it will be okay. I believe that's what the Psalmist was trying to drive home when he wrote,

> *"Take delight in the Lord, and He will give you your heart's desires." (Psalm 37:4)*

It doesn't say build up desires in your heart and then go to God, asking Him to "perform" these things for you. It says to delight in the Lord, the same Lord who we should strive to know intimately. As Larry Crabb wrote in his book *Shattered Dreams*,

> *"Shattered dreams are never random. They are always a piece in a larger puzzle, a chapter in a larger story. The Holy Spirit uses the pain of shattered dreams to help us discover our desire for God, to help us begin dreaming the highest dream. They are ordained opportunities for the Spirit to awaken, then to satisfy our highest dream."*[8]

If the total sum of your life is pursuing something you came up with on your own, you are going to find yourself empty time and time again. But if your number one goal is knowing God and following Him wherever He leads, your life is going to ignite in a way you could have never imagined.

For you it may mean surrendering your dreams only to watch God plant new ones in your heart and soul. For others it may mean watching as God takes the seed of a dream that has been planted in their heart and turn it into a reality. Not because of something super spiritual we did, but more-so because of something that does in us.

The closer we grow to God, the more we become like Him. And the more we become like Him, the more our hearts reflect His. And the more our hearts reflect His, the more our desires mimic His.

As we connect with the King of Kings and Lord of Lords, our hearts change. That doesn't necessarily mean all of the dreams, goals and plans we have disappear, but rather those dreams, goals and plans that are of ourselves and not of Him fade away.

So if your dream for your future is to start a youth ministry in your hometown and the closer you grow to God the more the flame gets fanned into fire, it's not something to be ignored.

Or if you never thought twice about the travesty it is that today thousands of people are dying of hunger around the world and now, the closer you get to God, you can't get that thought off your heart or mind, then take stock.

When it comes to our lives, God doesn't leave us in the dark. Rather as we walk with Him, He whispers to us gently. Sometimes these whispers come across more as shouts, through obvious encounters or divine door slams. Other times they drift gently into our lives and without a little magnification, we may miss out on them.

It could be the email we got from a complete stranger which just seems to line up with everything else that's going on around us.

It could be the conversation we had with a friend when their words were shouting across our souls, confirming what we've been suspecting for some time.

It could be the book we randomly pick up only to find the page we're reading sounds like it might have been written specifically for us in this given moment of time.

It could be the Bible verse the pastor reads before the start of his sermon that seems to have had your name on it.

All of these instances are not to be ignored, but rather weighed carefully. God speaks to all of us in many different ways. Sometimes through a sunset, or even through a stranger, He speaks and He moves in more ways than we could ever hope to imagine.

You might not be expecting it. You might not even know what the message means at the moment, but whatever you do, don't ignore the whisper of God when it comes singing softly in your life.

It might not be singing a message you are familiar with. What you're hearing might sound a little crazy or scary at first. But as you seek God and chase after Him with everything you've got, you can know that not only is He going to guide you, He's going to give you exactly what you need to walk in the direction that He leads.

I'm ashamed to say there was a period of time in my life when I doubted that God would give me what I needed to get where He was leading me. As I mentioned, for years I battled with sleeping disorders and health problems which have left me feeling chronically fatigued.

Instead of waking up to face the day, ra, ra, and raring to go, I struggle to climb out of bed and I usually spend the first few hours of my day in a fog. My engine would run very differently than that of a healthy person. You might start the day with 100 energy points you can use up before your head hits the pillow, where I on the other hand might have only had as many as 60 on a good day.

Knowing this reality, I seriously doubted for quite some time I was capable of doing the things I firmly believed God was calling me to do. Deep down inside I knew that with only as many as 60 points to give, the math just wasn't going to work.

I mean I had to use some points on daily living and everything which comes with that.

A big chunk needed to be invested in my job.

Others would be needed for the radio show I host and produce — the MAD Christian Radio Show.

Then let's not forget about Thursday night and the College and Careers group I led at the time.

There was also maintaining relationships with friends and family.

And how in the world would I still find enough points left over to work on this book — something I believed in with all my heart and knew beyond all reason, God was calling me to write?

No matter how many different ways I tried to add it up, I was coming up severely short. Yet there was nothing on that list I was able to cut.

However an amazing thing happened when I took my attention off of this problem and instead focused on God. What I needed always seemed to come in the right time. There was no way to explain it other than to know and recognize it was a God thing.

Many evenings I would be so tired I had to leave the dinner table, but would miraculously perk up just before it was time for College and Careers.

There were days when I could barely keep my eyes open, but some way, somehow I was able to focus on finishing what needed to be done for work.

Several times my speech was slurred and scrambled because of exhaustion, yet somehow I got enough clarity to be able to record the radio show.

Isaiah chapter 40 became my favorite as I witnessed it's words unfold into truth in my life,

> "O Jacob, how can you say the Lord does not see your troubles? O Israel, how can you say God ignores your rights? Have you never heard? Have you never understood? The Lord is the everlasting God,

> *the Creator of all the earth. He never grows weak or weary. No one can measure the depths of his understanding. He gives power to the weak and strength to the powerless. Even youths will become weak and tired, and young men will fall in exhaustion. But those who trust in the Lord will find new strength. They will soar high on wings like eagles. They will run and not grow weary. They will walk and not faint."*
> *(Isaiah 40:27-31)*

God provided just what I needed at the exact moment I needed it. It doesn't make sense nor is it something that I can explain exactly, but it's something that I know beyond all doubt.

Energy is something that I required and it was provided. On the other hand your need might not be energy, it could be you're in need of skills or talent or time or money. It doesn't matter what the need is because it's the same Jehovah-Jireh, the provider, that we follow.

Whether your need is courage, strength, money, time, encouragement, or guidance, God is going to provide you with exactly what you need, exactly in His perfect timing, for His exact purposes.

God's got an amazing plan for all of our lives and when we take our plans off the throne and instead place Him there, we are going to see some amazing events unfold. It may not be the way we pictured it, but it will be exactly the way He's writing it.

CHAPTER SEVEN

You're Still Here

> *"My Lord God, I have no idea where I am going. I do not see the road ahead of me. I cannot know for certain where it will end. Nor do I really know myself, and the fact that I think I am following Your will does not mean that I am actually doing so. But I believe that my desire to please You does in fact please You... And I know that if I do this You will lead me by the right road though I may know nothing about it. Therefore will I trust you always though I may seem to be lost and in the shadow of death."*
>
> — THOMAS MERTON

August 3, 2009 was a very eventful day in the McNulty household. While my Mom and I were video chatting with my sister Erin, who lived in Souther Ontario at the time, her phone rang with the news that my brother Trevor and his then fiancée, now wife, Hannah were in a car accident. Erin didn't get a lot of details but we did know that after being sideswiped by a transport truck their car went off the road. Miraculously both Trevor and Hannah were okay.

It would be shocking in a normal situation to get such a call but adding to the shock was the fact that less than two months before Trevor and Hannah were in another accident when they were hit by a moose and their lives were spared. Yes you read that right, hit by a moose. A moose literally ran into the side of their car, welcome to life in Northern Ontario.

Same two people. Two terrible accidents. Two miraculous outcomes!

While we were thanking and praising God for protecting the both of them, we were all very much aware the phone call coming after the accident could have been filled with tragic news. However on August 3, 2009 that was not the story for our family. It was not due to being spiritual gurus with an infallible hedge of protection around our family. It was as a result of God, in His infinite wisdom, knew both Trevor and Hannah had unfinished work to be done on this earth. His purpose for their lives wasn't completed yet so they were spared.

The truth of the matter is God has numbered all of our days. The Bible tells us,

> *"You saw me before I was born.*
> *Every day of my life was recorded in Your book.*
> *Every moment was laid out*
> *before a single day had passed." (Psalm 139:16)*

If you're still breathing it means God's purpose for you here on this earth has not been completed yet.

It doesn't matter how badly the scenery on the road of your life has looked so far or how many doors have slammed shut, you're here for a very specific reason.

The people around you, the job you hold, the groups you're involved with, the neighbors you talk to while watering the garden (or in my case, washing the car), are no accident.

> *"We can make our own plans,*
> *but the Lord gives the right answer.*
> *People may be pure in their own eyes,*

> *but the Lord examines their motives.*
> *Commit your actions to the Lord,*
> *and your plans will succeed.*
> *The Lord has made everything for His own purposes,*
> *even the wicked for a day of disaster."*
> *(Proverbs 16:1-4)*

Don't you love that truth? God has made everything for His own purposes. Everything around us, everything we see near or far, everything we touch is all part of a bigger purpose. If you are still breathing your story hasn't reached the end. What's around you is simply another chapter being written in your life story.

Whether you're wandering through a wilderness like the Israelites, stuck in the stomach of a whale like Jonah, or waiting for your emergence from a tomb like Jesus, God's still got a plan that is being carried out in your life. The problem is all too often we mistake a lack of visible movement as a cue for us to become complacent. Which is the worst possible thing that we can do.

In Matthew 25, we find three guys who find themselves in this boat. They are all waiting. Their master has gone away. They don't know when he will be back or what he's coming back with. All they know is the day will come when he returns,

> *"Again, the Kingdom of Heaven can be illustrated by the story of a man going on a long trip. He called together his servants and entrusted his money to them while he was gone. He gave five bags of silver to one, two bags of silver to another, and one bag of silver to the last—dividing it in proportion to their abilities. He then left on his trip." (Matthew 25:14-15)*

These servants were given a choice. Do they stand around twiddling their thumbs until he comes back with the next big and great thing? Or do they crack down and do what they can with what they've been given in the meantime?

It would be a wonderful story if all three of them had sprung into action, but that's not what happens. While the first and second servant decided to not be complacent in their waiting time, the third servant went ahead and buried his gold. He did absolutely nothing with it and waited and waited and waited some more.

While at the time this servant might have looked like he had it made to anyone passing by, he was forgetting something very important — what we're given we're expected to use. It doesn't matter if our master is standing over our shoulder or not. It doesn't make a difference if we don't feel like we're supposed to be in this in between time or not. It doesn't take into account how we feel about our position at the moment. If we have something, and each one of us does, this story teaches us we had better be doing something with it.

The third servant learned this lesson the hard way when the master finally returned. He called his servants together to give an account of what they had done with what they had been given. When the first two servants were called up, they were both able to give the report that they had invested their gold and had doubled the money. As a result, both earned the same praise from their master,

> *"Well done, my good and faithful servant. You have been faithful in handling this small amount, so now I will give you many more responsibilities. Let's celebrate together!" (Matthew 25:21)*

But the third servant didn't hear those wonderful words of praise. Instead, after admitting he was afraid to lose the money and thus buried it, he was told,

> "But the master replied, 'You wicked and lazy servant! If you knew I harvested crops I didn't plant and gathered crops I didn't cultivate, why didn't you deposit my money in the bank? At least I could have gotten some interest on it.' Then he ordered, 'Take the money from this servant, and give it to the one with the ten bags of silver. To those who use well what they are given, even more will be given, and they will have an abundance. But from those who do nothing, even what little they have will be taken away.'"
> (Matthew 25:26-29)

When I read this story, I learn many lessons from it. However one of the lessons that stands out most in my mind is we are all called to be investing on God's behalf at all times. It doesn't matter if we are afraid to fail, if we're in a place in life we're not too happy with or if our world is spinning out of control. Everyone of us has been given something at this point in time we are called to invest.

You might be waiting for the day when you can go to Bible college to be a youth pastor, but what's stopping you from using your gift with the youth at your church here and now?

You may be wanting to start a campaign to raise money to build a well in Africa, but what's stopping you from sending some of your own money over in the meantime?

You might be dreaming of using your God-given music gift to record an album and go out on tour, but what's stopping you from sharing your music now? At church? In your community? With your family and friends?

Your heart's desire might be for kids and you might not have children of your own, but what's stopping you from getting involved in a children's ministry at church or becoming a mentor to a child who could really use some guidance?

I once heard it said a Christian never retires and that's so true. No matter what stage of life you're in or what obstacles you're having to overcome, you've been given something to invest in God's kingdom.

That's not what Satan would have us believe though. Satan will try to sell us any lie and he will put up any roadblock he can to stop us from investing what we've been given, because as the story teaches us, anything invested in God's kingdom yields a return. The only thing which produces nothing is the gifts that are buried.

That's why Satan works overtime trying to convince us to live life like the third servant. He tries to trick us into believing that just because we haven't "arrived" where we thought we'd be, it's an excuse to operate on spiritual cruise control. In reality, the truth is if we're not investing our gifts now when times are tough, we're not going to be prepared to invest them when times are great either. Obedience to God is a lifelong process that has to be practiced in the valleys, the mountaintops, and the deserts.

We see that in the life of the first servant. He was given the most and he could have easily slacked off and not doubled his amount. In the end, even without receiving any interest, he would have had more than the other servants. However according to the parable he worked just as hard. His master asked him, he responded, no ifs, ands, or buts about it.

Wherever you are, whatever you have, you are called to be faithful with whatever you've been given. This is illustrated in one of my favorite quotes, found on the back of a HM (Hard Music) Magazine:

> *"David was the youngest son of a shepherd, but he became the greatest king of Israel. Paul ardently persecuted the early church, but he became the one who would spread the Gospel to the Gentiles. Mary was an ordinary teenage girl who became the mother*

> *of the Messiah. There are times in our lives when things seem almost hopeless but God wants to use us all for great purposes. He does not look at our current condition, but at what we have the potential to become. We should view others and ourselves in the same way... We should try to view all things with faith and hope that God can and will transform us into the people He wants us to be."*

All of the people mentioned in this inspiring quote have something pretty powerful in common — they didn't start their lives up on the mountaintop. Instead they were faithful where they did start — in the valleys and the deserts. As a result, God was able to use them in pretty amazing ways! As those times in the valleys and deserts prepared them for what God had waiting for them.

David was the least in his clan. He was just a shepherd alone in the fields. But it was in those fields he was being prepared to slay a giant.

Mary was from a poor family, part of an oppressed people, living in a disrespected area of her country. But it was living in that oppressed and disrespected area that produced in Mary a faith so strong she believed where most of us would have only doubted.

We need to shift our focus and stop looking at these periods in our lives like a waiting room outside of an operating room where very little gets accomplished. Rather we should look at these times as if they are spent on the operating table where the Great Physician is producing in us what we need for the next section of the road.

Unlike a traditional surgeon, Jesus doesn't use an anesthetic when He does His work and neither should we. Instead of sleepwalking through life, numbing ourselves in the process, we need to embrace every moment and make the most of every opportunity. Erwin McManus wrote in Chasing Daylight,

> *"Even if everyone around you chooses to sleep, you must resist the temptation to join their slumber. Wake up! Get out of bed. God wants to change the world through your life if only you'll just do something."*[9]

So will you get out of bed every morning and remind yourself that each moment of your day has purpose? Will you live your life in such a way that whether you are talking to a potential employer or the person serving your coffee, you see it as a divine moment in time?

You have a story to tell, a Gospel to share and a world around you of people need to reach out to. You can very well choose to stay hidden at home because you feel you're no longer qualified due to a closed door, or you could stop feeling sorry for yourself, take a step of faith to march out to wherever God is leading and share His love with whoever you come across along the way!

God is doing great things all around us. The question is whether we're ready to take off our blinders and become a part of it. He doesn't force us to, but He does offer a great reward for those who do.

When your life passes on, will you be standing before Him fumbling up excuses for a lack of investment? Or will you be able to stand tall with tears running down your cheeks as He welcomes you home with the words, "Well done, good and faithful servant." What will happen then is influenced by what we do today.

CHAPTER EIGHT

Results Can Be Deceiving

> *"Oh, young man, character is worth more than money, character is worth more than anything else in this wide world."*
> — D.L. MOODY

In June of 2013 I found myself in the Toronto area for almost a week. I had tickets to a concert in the city on Saturday but decided to head down the Monday before to enjoy a little vacation in the days leading up to the show. After spending a few days east of the city with outstanding friends and their adorable newborn son, I took the train back into downtown Toronto and checked into my hotel.

Leading up to this trip I had really prayed God would present me with opportunities to share His love. But wouldn't you know it, even though my heart was there, nothing was happening. On Thursday I had even specifically wandered around Dundas Square, in the hopes of finding people I could reach out to. Wouldn't you know it, but minutes after arriving it started raining, sending people scurrying for shelter. After coming up empty, and getting soaked in the process, I headed back to my hotel thinking sharing God's love wasn't going to happen on this trip. However on Friday night it all changed and so did my preconception of what being used by God really looks like.

After spending the day with my brother, sister-in-law and nephew who were in the area for my brothers work training, I walked them back to their van just as the sun started to fade. After parting with them, I found myself walking past the Rogers Centre back towards my hotel and out of the corner of my eye I saw a woman sitting alone on the sidewalk. Knowing I needed to talk to her, but having no idea what I was going to say, I kept praying for God to give me words as my feet closed the gap between us. When I finally reached her I mumbled out the first line which came to mind, "can I pray for you?"

She looked stunned as I said that but no more stunned as I felt. I didn't know if I had just made a huge blunder which would send her running from me first and faith second. It only took a few seconds for her face to soften and the words to come out of her mouth uttering, "this never happens", followed by tears welling in her eyes. And she wasn't the only one with tears.

For the next few minutes as people passed us by on that busy walkway, I found myself down on the concrete with my new friend sharing names and concerns and hopes for the future. When it was time to walk away I smiled, shook her hand and promised to pray for her to find affordable housing.

As I left the encounter the question in my mind wasn't "did I do the right thing?", but rather "how blessed am I to have this opportunity?". That night I learned once again that being Jesus to the world isn't about doors opening and closing in our lives. It's about watching for opportunities around us and then taking the step of faith needed to love on people in whatever ways we can, whichever ways God leads us.

And He does lead us. Wouldn't you know it, after the concert on the next night with 45,000 people streaming out of the Rogers Centre who would I get a glimpse of from the corner of my eye but the same woman from the night before? Moving through the crowd towards her, goosebumps were shooting up and down my body as I became very much aware this was one of Jesus' encounters — His holy moments here on this earth.

Her face lit up when her eyes met mine. There in the middle of a packed crowd with people pushing and shoving to get to their cars or catch a train, she shared with me God was already answering the prayer uttered and repeated for less than 24 hours. She was contacted by the city housing authority, it looked like they had an opening for her!

Down on my knees on that sidewalk I repeated the words the Holy Spirit was impressing on my heart. I told her God heard the prayers, that He loved her and that even when things seem dark, He does have a plan for her life.

We parted ways that night with both of us having been brought out of the mundane of the everyday and into something I'm sure neither of us will ever forget. This was a moment when heaven touched earth and God allowed the two of us to be a part of it.

Now that I'm back home in Timmins, I realize I may never know the long term impact of that day on this side of heaven. However I do know that all around us God is writing a grand story of His love and He invites us to let our lives fill the pages.

You may feel as though you are somehow inferior because you haven't arrived at some sort of destination you had in mind or because you feel your role is too small in the grand scheme of things. Never forget that sometimes the smallest things have the biggest impact and sometimes the ones who doubt if they are making a difference at all create the biggest tidal waves of change. Listen to what Paul had to say about it in his letter to the church in Corinth,

> *"Remember, dear brothers and sisters, that few of you were wise in the world's eyes or powerful or wealthy when God called you. Instead, God chose things the world considers foolish in order to shame those*

> *who think they are wise. And he chose things that are powerless to shame those who are powerful. God chose things despised by the world, things counted as nothing at all, and used them to bring to nothing what the world considers important. As a result, no one can ever boast in the presence of God." (1 Corinthians 1:26-29)*

This isn't a concept we're used to running on — especially in our boastful society, where we base everything on appearances and results. From the size of our houses to the amount of our paycheck to the score on our golf card to the amount of friends we have on our social networking accounts, we are driven with a desperate need to impress those around us based on the external.

We often want nothing more than to outperform and impress people around us. As a result of this way of living, we carry this mentality into our Christian walk as well. Seeing a video surpass a million views online, international ministries, packed crowds on Sunday mornings, and sold out tours are the accomplishments we talk about and give attention to. While there is nothing wrong with any of these outreaches, no ministry should be elevated above any other. And no person should be lifted up higher than another. As Billy Graham humbly commented, "At the cross we are all on level ground."

The person who spends 10 years in a lifestyle of witnessing to their neighbors without seeing any visible results is just as valuable to the body of Christ as the person who got the opportunity to talk about God last night on the evening news.

The person who spends 25 often thankless years chasing after children's attention in the Sunday school department is just as important as the person who leads us in worship on Sunday mornings.

The person who faithfully cuts the church lawn week after week is held in just as high esteem to God as the person who leads small group every Wednesday night.

We learn this in the New Testament,

> *"All of you together are Christ's body, and each one of you is a part of it." (1 Corinthians 12:27)*

Paul didn't write that only the worship leaders, pastors, and evangelists are a separate and necessary part of the body. He said that each and every one of us is a separate and necessary part of the body of Christ. Together we work for one goal — to advance the Kingdom. But not all of us have the same role.

Some of us have the same gift, but even then, we often have been given our own unique way of applying it and some are able to use their gifts in very creative ways.

My great friend Carole is one of those people. She and her husband have a busy household with two precious girls, but she doesn't let that stop her from using her gifts in creative and wonderful ways. After the earthquake and tsunami in Japan while many of us were wondering what we could do here on the other side of the world, Carole was out there organizing a prayer vigil and a fundraiser to allow people in our community to come together and do something to help this battered country. It was truly incredible to see how many people from all different faith backgrounds came out for it. When our town had a number of forrest fires in the area, threatening homes and property, Carole was out buying supplies to help out the firefighters battling the blaze and she was vocal in encouraging other people to do the same. Those are just two examples of the many out of the box ways Carole has found to use her gifts and you can do the same.

Imagine how weird the church would look like if everyone who had a gift of music traveled somewhere else to use it, leaving individual church congregations empty of musicians. Or if on Sunday morning we had twenty people up at the front leading worship but the kids ministry downstairs had no one to lead the kids in song.

We are united in Who we serve, but unique in the way we do so. The Apostle Paul wrote,

> "There are different kinds of spiritual gifts, but the same Spirit is the source of them all. There are different kinds of service, but we serve the same Lord. God works in different ways, but it is the same God who does the work in all of us. A spiritual gift is given to each of us so we can help each other." (1 Corinthians 12:4-7)

We've all been given a gift to use. Whether your gift is encouragement, helps, craftsmanship, teaching, healing, or being a prayer warrior, you're a vital part of the body of Christ and God has a unique role for you in the church.

Many Christians have a hard time believing that. As a result, they sit on the sidelines for far too long. The truth is, God wants to use you here and now to make a difference. It doesn't matter if you're in the desert or getting ready to climb the mountaintop God can do amazing things in and through your life right here and right now.

Look at Paul for example. He was in prison for preaching the Gospel. To the outside world it looked like this major obstacle in his life would shortchange Paul's gift for evangelism and for reaching his world for Christ. After all, Roman prisons weren't exactly popular spots for inmates to start church services.

Yes as Paul remained faithful to God even in the chains of a prison, God used him exactly where he was and exactly for God's purposes. We see this occur in Acts chapter 16 when Paul and Silas were being held captive in the inner dungeon of the jail, with their feet clamped in stocks to ensure they could not escape.

That jail must have been a very dark place to be in; however even in that place Paul and Silas refused to let their light flicker. Instead of having a pity party, these guys had a time of prayer and praise. As they were singing hymns, while the prisoners listened in, there was an earthquake and the jail was shaken to its very foundations. The doors of the cells flew open and the chains of each and every prisoner fell off.

Paul and Silas could have made a run for it, and who wouldn't have? But rather they stayed and witnessed to the jailer. They preached the Gospel to him and not only was he saved, but all the members of his household came to believe and were baptized. The scriptures tell us,

> *"He and his entire household rejoiced because they all believed in God." (Acts 16:34)*

This all went down in a place many of us would have considered a pointless detour in their journey towards a destination. But Paul certainly didn't. Later on in Philippians he writes,

> *"And I want you to know, my dear brothers and sisters, that everything that has happened to me here has helped to spread the Good News. For everyone here, including the whole palace guard, knows that I am in chains because of Christ. And because of my imprisonment, most of the believers here have gained confidence and boldly speak God's message without fear." (Philippians 1:12-14)*

Due to an "unfair" imprisonment, many people heard about Christ and they were encouraged to be more bold in their faith in a dark place. A place where the name of Christ might not have been spoken otherwise.

The fact of the matter is, God doesn't make mistakes. He knows where we are supposed to be and at what point in our lives. He is well aware of how He's going to use us in that place.

Meanwhile, no matter how God ends up using us during the "in between" times of our lives, we all have the opportunity to be part of something especially powerful during these times. And that is the shaping of our character.

Often it's during the more difficult times in life or the times where we have no idea where we're headed we grow the most. I know I wouldn't be the person I am today without both the storms and the deserts that I've walked through. There is a special sort of growth that occurs in these places that just doesn't seem to happen when the sun is shining brightly and our worlds are nearly perfect.

Our character is the very cornerstone of who we are. Until we've allowed our character to be shaped by the God of all creation, we won't be properly equipped to walk through this life and all of the challenges that come during both the good times and the bad.

Shaping our character is something of the upmost importance to God, as we can see unfolding in the Bible, but it's also something that needs to be of the upmost importance to us. As it says in 1 Corinthians 13:1-3,

> *"If I could speak all the languages of earth and of angels, but didn't love others, I would only be a noisy gong or a clanging cymbal. If I had the gift of prophecy, and if I understood all of God's secret plans and possessed all knowledge, and if I had such faith that I could move mountains, but didn't love others, I would be nothing. If I gave everything I have to the poor and even sacrificed my body, I could boast about it; but if I didn't love others, I would have gained nothing."*
> *(1 Corinthians 13:1-3)*

We could lead worldwide ministries, engage hundreds of atheists in dialogue about God, feed all the poor, help turn our nations back to God, be part of a miraculous healing, but if we didn't carry the loving character of Christ with us and in us, it would be useless.

Knowing that, maybe it's time we placed a little less emphasis on where we are going and a little more emphasis on who we are becoming. If we look throughout the Bible, we see that there are many more verses that talk about our character than there are that talk about our calling. That's because, as we learned in those verses in 1 Corinthians, without living out the character of Christ anything we do is done in vain.

Like the potter molding the clay or the blacksmith refining the gold, God wants to work on shaping us into the people who He created us to be.

People who passionately love those around them.

People who have great patience even when the line-up seems to be moving slower than molasses in January.

People who are willing to walk the extra mile, do the extra job, take on the extra load.

People who don't keep a closet full of masks but are sincere to the core.

People who are willing to give up their rights and their desires to put others first.

People who are determined to live a life reflecting the light of Christ instead of launching themselves in the spotlight.

The truth of the matter is, character is one of the most important thing we can build while we're on this earth. We can be part of the biggest and greatest ministry this world has ever seen, but unless our character is in tact, everything is going to fall apart.

Flipping over to Ephesians, we see this idea shouted loud and clear when Paul writes,

> *"Therefore I, a prisoner for serving the Lord, beg you to lead a life worthy of your calling, for you have been called by God." (Ephesians 4:1)*

Paul doesn't say I beg you to live out your calling. He says I beg you to lead a life worthy of your calling. There is a big difference between the two when both are not simultaneously lived out.

Those who attempt to live out the calling without trying to live out a life worthy of the calling often find themselves trapped in the cycle of hypocrisy because without living out the life of the One we are called to serve, we're sending a false message.

So what does living out a life worthy of the calling look like? Paul gives us the answer in the following verses,

> *"Always be humble and gentle. Be patient with each other, making allowances for each other's faults because of your love. Always keep yourselves united in the Holy Spirit, binding yourselves together with peace." (Ephesians 4:2-3)*

Ultimately living a life worthy of the calling involves taking out the "I" and replacing it with Him. Since try as hard as we might, we're not going to be humbled, gentle, patient and people of unity if we're caught up in our own little worlds where we are the most important part of the equation. As long as we're obsessed with self, it isn't going to happen.

However when we take ourselves out of the number one spot and replace us with Him, an amazing thing happens. Where once we were caught up in making sure we get everything we think we are entitled to, we're now more concerned about His glory and the lifting up of His name.

In a practical sense it translates into lives of people who look, think, and act so much like Jesus that the world can't help but notice. People may be able to ignore our church or our crusades, but when someone unselfishly loves another or lays down their lives for the cause of Christ, it's going to catch some attention. And not attention in the way Hollywood teaches us it looks like "hey,

hey, look at me", but attention that screams out "hey, hey, look at Him!".

Jesus affirmed,

> *"Your love for another will prove to the world that you are my disciples." (John 13:35)*

He didn't ask us to post billboards. He didn't ask us to get t-shirts made. He asked us to love. And love is enough.

CHAPTER NINE

For Such a Time as This

"The truth is, of course, that what one regards as interruptions are precisely one's life."
— C.S. LEWIS

Hands down one of the best things in my life is a little guy who I affectionately refer to as Timmy-Tim-Tim, Timbucktoo, or sometimes Timbits. He is my nephew Timothy.

I've always loved kids and knew becoming an aunt would be a great experience. I had no idea though how much it would change me and change me it has.

At family dinners instead of sitting around the table with the adults I often will find myself sitting on the floor pushing around trucks with the little guy.

When I'm shopping I'll often end up in the toy aisles or children's clothing sections, finding (and yes buying) treasures I know he'll love.

It's caused my silly side to come out as Timmy and I will face off and do crazy things to make the other person laugh hysterically. Such as pretending to eat and then throw up his stuffed animals. He'll tease me by calling me "Auntie Choo Choo Train" or "Auntie Twisten" when he knows very well I'm Auntie Kristen. And I'll return the favor by calling him Mortimer.

Mostly it's awakened a love in me I didn't know was there. With this protective kind of love I would do anything to keep him safe and happy. I would give whatever I own to help meet a need he might have. It's a kind of love I'm sure is only a fraction of the love that parents feel for their children or what God feels for us.

In the days leading up to Timmy's birth in December of 2010 our entire family was filled with expectation as we awaited his arrival. Did he ever make us wait! My sister-in-law Hannah blew right by her due date and reached the point where the doctor decided it was time to induce. My mom, my sister Erin and her husband John, Hannah's parents and I planted ourselves at the hospital waiting for the little one to make his or her appearance. After inducing it was supposed to be a quick process, but with this little one it was more like start, stop, start, stop, start and stop again. Trevor and Hannah were both troopers, but they must have been exhausted after hours upon hours of stop and go.

Finally around midnight when labour had stalled again they were advised to rest for a couple of hours and we were advised to go home as it didn't look like the baby would be coming anytime soon. My mom, feeling great anticipation over the arrival of her first grandchild, decided to stay at the hospital. The rest of us headed home for the comfort of warm beds on that cold winter night.

Erin and John quickly fell asleep on the pull out couch in my rec room and while they were catching zzz's I was still very much wide awake, the byproduct of battling with terrible insomnia. I finally fell asleep around 3:30 am, only to be woken up by a phone call shortly after 4:00 am that we should come quick. It was time to push.

Immediately I sprang out of bed, got dressed and after making sure Erin and John were awake, ran outside to start the car. Unfortunately with the temperature hovering at -30 Celsius the locks were frozen, forcing me to literally crawl through the trunk and into the back seat just to get the doors unlocked and the car running. Nothing was going to stop me from being there for the birth of this baby.

Full of adrenaline I ran back into the house only to find Erin and John were both still in bed sleeping! I couldn't believe it! I quickly became their least favorite person as I flipped on all the lights and started yelling, "Let's go, let's go!!!!"

After what seemed to be an eternity they stumbled to the back door and then we were faced with a dilemma.

Erin with her eyes still half shut declared she couldn't drive. And John with fog clouding his mind said he probably shouldn't either.

I had willingly stopped driving for a while at that time as with my insomnia issues I was too tired during the day to be alert enough to get behind the wheel. But at this hour my body was raring to go so I grabbed the keys and jumped behind the wheel.

Once we were nearly at the hospital Erin woke up enough to realize "Oh my goodness, look Kristen's driving!" She grabbed the video camera and hit record. There is actually a clip of her panning the camera at me and I'm saying, "Years of insomnia have prepared me for this very moment."

At the time it was laughable, but in the years since I've thought a lot about that statement. The idea that years of something that I complained about and wished I didn't have could possibly prepare me for a moment that I would have never pictured.

I'm not actually saying I believe God allowed me to have insomnia for years so I could drive for a few minutes in order to reach the hospital in time for my nephew's birth. A taxi could have easily done the trick. But I do very much believe that those years weren't for nothing. Neither was the year and a half when I was feeling okay. Or the time now when I'm struggling with health issues again.

I'm starting to see that everything, and I mean everything, in our lives can serve to prepare us for what comes next.

We see this in the life of Esther as recounted in the Bible.

Some would say the deck was stacked against Esther from day one. She was an orphan, as both of her parents had passed away, leaving her to face the world without the guidance of a mom or dad. Thankfully, Esther's cousin Mordecai ended up taking Esther under his wing and he raised her as a Jew in Persia.

Now being a Jew in that time period wasn't a popular group to find yourself associated with. Outside powers tried time and time again to eliminate the Jewish race completely. While they had not yet completely succeeded, as a Jew you still didn't want to make waves.

Enter King Xerxes. As King of Persia, he was recently embarrassed by his wife, the Queen, when she refused to come to him when he sent for her. Instead of having it out with his wife like a normal couple would do, he decided to replace her. In an effort to prove to the outside world that he was still the man, the King sent out letters to all of the empire insisting that every man is the ruler of his own home and can say whatever he pleases.

It's one thing to approach a King with a different view under normal circumstances, but to do so when he made it crystal clear that he would not stand for the opinions and desires of others, particularly women, made for some pretty extreme circumstances for Esther to be called into. And called she was.

In an attempt to fill the void that the Queen had left, the King's personal attendants started a search for the most beautiful young women in the land so they could present them to the King. Esther was chosen as one of these women.

Hiding her Jewish background, in a land with no one but Mordecai in her court, Esther caught the eye of the King. In fact, King Xerxes was so impressed by her, he forgot about the other women vying for his eye and declared her to be the Queen.

So unknown to a nation, their Queen and the King of Persia's wife, was actually a Jew. It's not everyday a commoner is welcomed into the King's courts, let alone chosen as his wife. But God had a plan.

First of all He had a plan to save the King's life. When Mordecai heard of a plot to assassinate the King he was quick to report it to

Esther who passed the information along to the King. Thus, his life was spared.

Secondly God had a plan to save the Jews.

In the same time period, a man named Haman was promoted to prime minister of the nation. This made him the second most powerful man in the kingdom. But Haman was power hungry and when Mordecai refused to bow to him he decided to take out his rage on all of the Jews in the empire. Because he had the ear of King Xerxes, Haman was given a green light to kill all of the Jews in the land.

When Mordecai learned of this plot to kill his people he was understandably devastated. As the news spread to other Jews in the kingdom, they went into mourning. Who could blame them? Through the ego of one man they were all going to be put to death.

But Mordecai and the Jewish people had one last glimmer of hope — Esther. She was the only one in the land with even a chance of convincing the King to put a stop to Haman's plan.

Mordecai got a message about what was going to happen passed onto Esther. While she was saddened for her people, she was scared to take action and rightfully so. It was common practice that anyone who appeared before the King without invitation would be doomed to death unless the King held out his gold scepter. Since the King had not called for Esther in quite some time she was afraid to suddenly approach him with any kind of request. But Mordecai responded to her fears with the kind of wisdom we all would do well to keep in mind. He remarked,

> *"If you keep quiet at a time like this, deliverance and relief for the Jews will arise from some other place, but you and your relatives will die. Who knows if perhaps you were made queen for just such a time as this?" (Esther 4:14)*

Mordecai saw past the moment and realized Esther holding the position of Queen was no coincidence. He looked at the situation and saw God's hand in placing Esther in the palace. He was convinced this was her time to act and he was right.

Esther approached the King and the King not only spared her life by holding out the scepter, but also saved the lives of all of the Jews in the kingdom after hearing what Esther had to say. Haman was defeated and killed. Mordecai was promoted in his place and the Jews were saved with a new decree protecting their lives.

Only God could orchestrate for a young orphan to rise to the position of Queen in a land that didn't belong to her people. For such a time as this.

Maybe you're reading this and you can clearly see God's hand in Esther's life, but you're having trouble seeing it in your story. Let me say it and it's my prayer that you believe it — the same God who orchestrated Esther's life has your life in His hands. The situation might look bleak, the promises may be fading from your mind; however your story is still being written with more depth and beauty than you can see from where you are right now.

Sometimes we, like Esther, will be able to look back and clearly see how the circumstances of our lives build to such a beautiful crescendo. Or look back and put together how one experience combined with another took us to a remarkable place with a remarkable plan But there will be times in our lives when we can't see any of those things. Nonetheless we can't for one moment think that just because we can't see the purpose means there is none.

Hebrews chapter 11 has been painted the "hall of faith" when it comes to the men and women we read about in the Bible. In that chapter we find the stories summarized of many who have gone before us and did amazing things with their lives. We read about Gideon, Samson and David who ruled nations, conquered armies, and brought kingdoms back to God. While these men could look back and recognize the movement of God's hand guiding them through unfavorable moments with a purpose in mind, the story doesn't end there. Hebrews 11 gives us a very clear picture that not all the heroes of the faith of the past or of today are going to have a life where all the puzzle pieces visibly fit together,

> *"How much more do I need to say? It would take too long to recount the stories of the faith of Gideon, Barak, Samson, Jephthah, David, Samuel, and all the prophets. By faith these people overthrew kingdoms, ruled with justice, and received what God had promised them. They shut the mouths of lions, quenched the flames of fire, and escaped death by the edge of the sword. Their weakness was turned to strength. They became strong in battle and put whole armies to flight. Women received their loved ones back again from death. But others were tortured, refusing to turn from God in order to be set free. They placed their hope in a better life after the resurrection. Some were jeered at, and their backs were cut open with whips. Others were chained in prisons. Some died by stoning, some were sawed in half, and others were killed with the sword. Some went about wearing skins of sheep and goats, destitute and oppressed and mistreated. They were too good for this world, wandering over deserts and mountains, hiding in caves and holes in the ground. All these people earned a good reputation because of their faith, yet none of them received all that God had promised."*
> *(Hebrews 11:32-39)*

Notice that last sentence,

"All these people earned a good reputation because of their faith, yet none of them received all that God had promised."

Your life and mine aren't always going to add up. Often we won't see the forest for the trees. We might spend a good deal of time on this earth wandering. While to the untrained eye, we look like nothing more than people who are aimlessly drifting, to God we look like His children who are living out the lives He planned for them.

God has reasons that are far beyond our understanding. If everything that happened on this earth made sense it wouldn't really make the case for a Creator since the creation could stand on its own apart from Him. But it is true. We have a Creator who has orchestrated kings and kingdoms, who has changed lives and nations, who has Himself died just so that we would always live. That's love, that's planning and that's the God who doesn't ask us to understand Him. He just asks us to trust and follow Him.

Esther did and found she reached a place where she could see her life was a dress rehearsal that led up to preparing her for a leading role as Queen.

Moses did and found his Jewish heritage and his childhood days in Pharaoh's palace collided to create just the right man for the job of setting God's people free.

Yet, Abraham did and never set foot in the promised land or met all of his descendants who God promised would outnumber the stars. However we know the end of that story. We know what Abraham's life on this earth meant in the grand scheme of things and how God fulfilled His promise to Abraham in the generations to come. Abraham never saw it, but it didn't make it not true.

So what about you? Will you follow with the same kind of faith?

Will you look at your past and even though you don't get it, surrender it?

Will you look at your present and even though you would have never picked it, choose to live it and live it fully?

Will you look towards your future and stop eying the goals you created and instead keep your eyes on the One who created you?

His timing might not be ours, but His promises are true. For such a time as this.

CHAPTER TEN

Surrendering Your Isaac

"There are far, far better things ahead than any we leave behind."
— C.S. LEWIS

Science may have advanced by leaps and bounds since the first days of creation, but infertility is still a huge problem which in some cases just cannot be fixed. Many of us know someone who has experienced the painful and gut-wrenching reality of not being able to bear a child. Maybe you have experienced the loss of that dream yourself.

If we turn back to the first pages of our Bibles, we find a couple who faced the same struggle.

Abram, also known as Abraham, and Sarah wanted nothing more than to have children. With every calendar year that passed in their marriage though, they were both forced to come face to face with the painful reality that having a child didn't seem likely. Talk about a closed door!

Yet Abram had been given something many of those who struggle with infertility never receive — a promise from God of a child who would be born to them,

> "Then the Lord said to him, 'No, your servant will not be your heir, for you will have a son of your own who will be your heir.' Then the Lord took Abram outside and said to him, 'Look up into the sky and count the stars if you can. That's how many descendants you will have!' And Abram believed the Lord, and the Lord counted him as righteous because of his faith." (Genesis 15:4-6)

It would be amazing if the story ended here on a happy note with a baby born nine months later, but it doesn't. Time was ticking and as time went on, Abram and Sarah started to doubt the validity of God's plan. After all, Sarah was getting up there in age and if they waited much longer, Abram's chances weren't going to be very good either. So they did what we all do when our trust in God starts to waver — they intervened.

Sarah sends one of her servants to sleep with her husband. Abram goes along with the disastrous plan and nine months later little Ishmael is born. While the story could have ended right there, God still had a plan for Sarah, Abram and their descendants. Instead of going with the human plan B, God made it clear to Abram that he wasn't finished with him yet,

> "What's more, I am changing your name. It will no longer be Abram. Instead, you will be called Abraham, for you will be the father of many nations. I will make you extremely fruitful. Your descendants will become many nations, and kings will be among them!" (Genesis 17:5-6)

One promise from God would be more than any one of us could hope for or expect. Yet this case God gave something more to Sarah and Abraham — He gave them His word again. And instead of abandoning them to their own plan B, He kept His word. In Genesis 18 we're told the Lord appeared to Abraham again and while Sarah was listening from a nearby tent, He told them that in a year Sarah would bear a son.

So what does Sarah do? Probably what most of us would do in the same situation — she laughs and then questions how this could possibly be. What was God's response? A question of His own,

> "Is anything too hard for the Lord?" (Genesis 18:14)

Finally the cry of a baby was heard in that Jewish household and a son was born with both Sarah and Abraham's DNA. When it came time to name their bundle of joy, Abraham and Sarah choose a name which spoke both of Sarah's reaction to the promise from God and represented what their son had brought them — Isaac, which translated means laughter.

Here we have two people who are more than likely on top of the world. The dream they thought was long ago dead was resurrected and joy filled their household through the birth of this miracle baby. After years of hopelessness and pain, hope filled their hearts and lives like rays of sunshine. So much so that Genesis tells us Abraham threw a big party to celebrate their good fortune.

It would be such a great Hollywood scene if the story ended here, but it doesn't. Instead of rolling the credits with the birth of Isaac, God has more pages scenes in the works.

Isaac grows up and likely, as a miracle child, is the apple of his parents eyes. The artist Rembrandt does a magnificent job of illustrating the relationship between father and son in his work of art titled "Abraham and Isaac." I saw this painting when I was at the Art Gallery of Ontario and I couldn't help but stop and stare at it for a good deal of time. In this masterpiece not only does Rembrandt display a brilliant amount of detail, he also captures an expression on Abraham's face that portrays the joy and pride this father had for his son.

Abraham and Sarah were given a second chance and a great joy. But just when life couldn't look better for this family, God tells Abraham the thing he values the most, the one thing which has held such promise and hope, is the very thing God is asking him to lay down.

Many of us have been asked to lay down jobs and dreams and relationships and circumstances on God's altar. Meanwhile God asked Abraham to lay down Isaac, his own flesh and blood, the very promise of God.

What surprises me about this story is Abraham's response. The God that he loves with all of his heart is asking him to offer his son as a human sacrifice. For a guy who doubted God the first time God mentioned a crazy idea, he certainly doesn't show much hesitation here. In fact we're told the very next morning Abraham got up early, saddled his donkey, got two of his servants and Isaac and went on his way to the mountain. He even brought along firewood for the burnt offering, which as far as he knows, is going to be his own son.

With every step he takes closer to the mountain that God directed him to, he must feel like bolting in the other direction. However, Abraham keeps walking and he keeps his son Isaac at his side. When he gets to the destination, he builds an altar. And when the altar is built, he ties up his own son, lays him on top of the wood and lifts up his knife.

Could you imagine the torment that must be filling this Abraham's soul? I'm not a parent, but even I could imagine the anguish someone would feel at the prospect of losing their own child and at their own hand at that! The despair, the fear, the doubt, the pain that Abraham must have been feeling can not be comprehended or captured with mere words. Meanwhile we're told at Abraham stood with knife raised, ready to give up the greatest thing that had ever happened to him, the very thing he loved the most.

Maybe after all of his struggles with doubt and trust, Abraham learned something we would all benefit to know — that even the greatest dreams and biggest promises aren't ours to hold onto. We might have been given a dream job, great family, fabulous ministry or once in a lifetime opportunity, but when God asks us to lay these things down, they are not ours to wrestle over. Instead they are ours to gently let go of and place into the hands of who they belong to — God.

I had to learn this lesson the hard way a few years ago. For nearly seven years of my life I was involved in a young adult's ministry, I was as an attendee first, then a leader. In many ways this group was like the promised fulfilled by God bringing hope and light into my life and allowing me to use my gifts to reflect His love here on earth.

I loved everything about the group and even during the dark days every ministry goes through, I felt much joy related to my involvement. Having the opportunity to prepare studies, plan parties and special events, disciple new believers, spend time building up with those who attended — it was like a dream come true. I felt like my gifts were being used and this was a place I really belonged.

You can imagine my great disappointment when I started to get the feeling God was asking me to lay this "Isaac" down. I resisted this idea with everything I had in me. Instead of listening to the message that the season was over and the life was gone from the group, I did everything but stand on my head (and only because I have a terrible sense of balance) to revitalize the group and bring some life back into our meetings. It was almost as if I thought if only I could find one spark of life that God wouldn't ask me to lay it down any more.

But that's not the truth we learn from Abraham. From Abraham we learn that sometimes God will ask us to raise a knife to even that which is alive and well.

After much wrestling with God and prayer and wise counsel from my pastor, I realized I needed to lay down what was never mine to hold onto. Sitting in my pastor's office one February afternoon, I resolved to stop running and instead do what God asked me to do.

Let's go back to Abraham. If you know the story, you know something remarkable happens here. Just as Abraham is about to sacrifice all he has to give, God intervenes. The Bible tells us that the angel of the Lord calls out to Abraham and Abraham immediately responds with "Yes, I'm listening." The angel goes on to tell him not to hurt Isaac and that this moment in time showed God that Abraham truly feared Him because he didn't hold back even that which was so precious. Then God goes on to give Abraham another truly awesome promise,

> *"Because you have obeyed me and have not withheld even your son, your only son, I swear by my own name that I will certainly bless you. I will multiply your descendants beyond number, like the stars in the sky and the sand on the seashore. Your descendants will conquer the cities of their enemies. And through your descendants all the nations of the earth will be blessed — all because you have obeyed me." (Genesis 22:16-18)*

Wow, what a story! And it didn't end there. Not only was Abraham sent home with his precious son in tow, but God sent a lamb to provide the sacrifice in Isaac's place. This was a marvelous blessing to Abraham and a beautiful foreshadowing of the Lamb, Jesus, who would make the ultimate sacrifice of His blood to cover our sins once and for all.

I wish I could tell you that the second we all raise the knives on our own "Isaac", so to speak, God would run in with something else to sacrifice, but that isn't always the case. Sometimes He provides a substitute; yet there are other times when we're called to bring the "knife" down on what He still holds in His hands.

That was the story for me with the College and Careers group. I kept waiting for God to provide something else or for Him to tell me this was only a test to see if I would be faithful, but after that afternoon in my pastor's office, God kept sending confirmation after confirmation that the time had come. It was now my turn to take a step of faith and obedience.

So on March 4, 2010 I sat in front of a group of unsuspecting young adults and told them we had reached the end of the road. It was one of the hardest things I've ever had to do in my life. While God didn't send a lamb to take the place of the sacrifice, He however did send some other pretty powerful blessings.

First of all He sent His peace. I once again was reminded of why the Bible describes God's peace as one that surpasses human understanding. In the time between when I made the decision and when I made the announcement to the group, peace was my constant companion. Where the natural Kristen thing to do would be to panic, freak out and doubt myself, there was no room for any of those things once God's peace entered my heart. Yes, I was concerned about how some members of the group might take the news. After all, I was giving them the shock of their week, possibly even their year. But I didn't doubt for a second it was the right thing to do.

Secondly, God sent some pretty amazing people to stand with me during this time. These friends were able to give me wise counsel and stand shoulder to shoulder with me as I walked into the room and said the words I didn't want to say. They encouraged me to follow where God leads and not worry about the rest. While they didn't see the whole picture yet either, they were filled with trust that this was the way to go. And they represented the love of Christ to me when I needed it the most.

In the days that followed I wish I could tell you I had some sort of life altering moment or complete understanding of why this had to happen. I didn't. Today I have inklings of why it needed to happen, but I don't know for sure. All the same I do know the words of Job are true,

> "The Lord gave me what I had, and the Lord has taken it away. Praise the name of the Lord." (Job 1:21)

We might never understand why we're asked to lay down what we cherish in our lives, even if they seem so good in and of themselves. But we can come to the place where our trust in the God who does the asking outweighs any fears or doubts that might try to cloud our hearts and souls. As we're about to learn though, that's not always the easiest thing to do when we are in the midst of the darkness before the dawn.

CHAPTER ELEVEN

The Darkness Before The Dawn

"I would rather walk with God in the dark than go alone in the light."
— MARY GARDINER BRAINARD

After years of being held captive in a huge desert in life because of my illness and sleeping problems, you can imagine my great relief when in May 2010 I finally felt like I was turning a corner.

I had tried many different sleeping medications over the course of my illness, but after traveling to Toronto to see some specialists, they suggested one that worked. I was finally getting eight hours of refreshing sleep every night! To say it was fantastic is the biggest understatement of the year!

Nights of tossing and turning were replaced with solid sleep. Days of lethargy and "brain fog" were filled with energy and clarity. Moments of having to say "no" to activity after activity were exchanged for the ability to say "yes" and enjoy things I had surrendered for years due to my health such as tennis, golf and basketball.

My personality changed too. Where before I was dull from my lack of sleep, now I was fired up and felt like I really came alive. This new lease on life was accompanied by excitement as I considered the endless possibilities for my future. You see, when

I was in the middle of my mess I didn't allow myself to think too much about the future since with a diagnosis of Chronic Fatigue Syndrome you never know when or if you are going to get better. That said, I had to become okay with not knowing and not planning too far ahead. My focus was getting through today and I couldn't allow myself to think very far beyond the day right in front of me.

Now with a sudden influx of energy I started thinking ahead and dreaming for the future. I rejoiced in the thought I would be able to start working full time again and with that would come financial freedom to travel, buy a car, and eventually a house. The sky was the limit and I was fully enjoying dreaming about the possibilities. It was as if a light switch had been turned on and I was determined to soak every ray of light in.

Unfortunately this great awakening came with a huge price tag I never considered or planned for. I have always been fairly stable when it comes to my emotions with not a lot of highs or lows – more of a constant cruise control. But then after a few weeks of taking my new medication and some trial and error to find the right dose, I noticed my emotions started fluctuating more than the stock market does.

These new emotional spikes caused the feeling of needing to cry at the drop of a hat. For some this might not be so foreign, but for me it was torture. I am not a crier. In fact I used to cry so little that I have had people purposefully try to make me cry just because they wanted to be the one to help "break the floodgates." With this medication the anti-crying Kristen was suddenly gone and I was having mini moments of losing it for no particular reason.

Then Satan came along and did what he does best — take advantage of you while you are down. I experienced a spiritual attack which was so strong and severe it made me question on many occasions if I was losing my mind. I mean, how can you go from being on the top of the world one week to spiraling out of control the next?

Well I was about to learn the lesson that if Satan can't get you when you are down, he's not going to stop trying once you are climbing up.

In my case Satan couldn't destroy me while I was wandering in the wilderness, but by taking the medication I did, I ended up giving him the open door he needed to try and take me down. While these pills did wonders with releasing melatonin to help me sleep, they also played havoc with serotonin, which controls your mood and emotions. If I was taking a low dose of the drug I would have been fine, but because I needed such a high dose to actually sleep it caused my emotions to go out of whack, leaving me spiraling into a depression. The medication was just the foothold that Satan was waiting for in order to try and bring me down. As anyone who has ever gone through a depression well knows, depression can lower your defenses and make you susceptible like few things can.

Often when things start to get better or we look ahead and see good things on the horizon, we get tempted to relax our guard. We get fooled into thinking the worst is behind us and now Satan is ready to forget about us. The reality could not be further from the truth.

My pastor told me once that Satan is a stalker. He observes us in every situation and he just waits for the perfect opportunity to put us in a tail spin. In my story the opportunity was medication which finally caused me to sleep but also caused my serotonin to get out of control. For you it might be completely different.

Your open door might be your deciding to move into a different job. Now Satan is using insecurity to make you second guess every decision you make.

Or maybe you've decided to take a leap of faith in a relationship and now Satan has you so scared about the possibility of getting hurt, you want to take your heart back before you even start to hand it over.

Or perhaps you have started leading a new ministry. Where once you walked with confidence; now Satan has you doubting yourself and your abilities. This has left you paralyzed with fear, leaving your ministry ineffective.

Satan is the master manipulator and the biggest enemy we will ever encounter in life. He is the ultimate predator, who makes it his business to know his prey and like a lion in the outback, he waits for the perfect moment to attack. And attack he does.

In my situation I became a completely different person. The ups and downs from the medication were one thing, but when these ups and downs would hit they were followed by a nonstop stream of lies.

Lies that I wasn't good enough.

Lies that I was not loved.

Lies that I was losing my mind and something was wrong with me.

Lies that I was going to lose my job, ministry, family, and friendships.

Lies that God had all but abandoned me.

Instead of going out there and enjoying my newfound energy, all I wanted to do was hide. And hide I did. I was so embarrassed about "the new me" that I disguised it from everyone I could. I put on a plastic smile, practiced the right lingo and did everything in my power to keep a shield up which would stop anyone from being able to see the mess I had unraveled into over the course of only a few weeks.

Thankfully it wasn't long before my mom and a friend both noticed something was wrong. I broke down and told them (after swearing them to secrecy) that the once "stable" Kristen had become an emotional basket case. But even though I told them, I still made a conscious decision to hide it from everyone else except for my pastor. I even went so far as to stop going out with people because I didn't want anyone to notice I was off my game.

In hindsight this was the worst decision I could have made at the time. My choice actually played right into the cards Satan was trying to deal. The enemy of our souls knows the power that exists in relationships and community. He knows it is through our connections with other Christians that we are fueled, inspired and transformed. So what better way to kick us when we're down than to encourage us to hide?

If that's the place you are in, I cannot encourage you enough to do the exact opposite. The only thing worse than being in complete darkness is being in complete darkness alone.

I don't know what I would have done without the unconditional love of my mom, the steadfast support of my friend and the wise counsel and guidance of my pastor. It's people who hold us up when we are weak, remind us we are not alone and can speak truth to counteract the lies Satan throws at us.

One of the lies I struggled with the most was the idea that God had somehow abandoned me. I felt like I was on my own in the fight; as if God had taken Satan off of his leash when it came to me.

I prayed so hard and wanted nothing more than for this darkness to retreat. When it didn't happen it became easy to confuse being in an uncomfortable place with being abandoned by God. I mistook the presence of darkness with the absence of light.

As a result I started to slip into the very darkness I had previously fought against. No matter how hard people tried to encourage me, I was trapped in a state of discouragement as a result of believing the lie that God had checked out on my situation and I was left to fight off this evil guy named Satan alone.

It got to its breaking point one Thursday night when I was at my friend's house. I went over before dinner and was planning to stay the evening, although I nearly left early because it was the worst hang out time we've ever had. I was depressed, she was very tired and no matter how hard she tried to shed light on my situation I wasn't allowing for anything but darkness. I couldn't feel God in the midst of this. As a result, no matter how hard she tried to encourage me that this was part of a greater plan and part of God preparing me to really use my gifts, I didn't want to acknowledge anything other than my pain.

I went upstairs, planning on leaving, but once I reached the top of the staircase the sun shining into the living room caught my eye. The angle of the sun sent rays cascading into the room and onto the study guide for the book "Fearless" by Max Lucado which was sitting on her coffee table. It was a book we were reading together, going through the study and discussion questions after each chapter we completed. However life had gotten busy and even though both of us had read the next chapter, we had slacked on doing the discussion.

While I was eying the book something deep down inside of me told me now was the time, so I asked if she was up for going ahead with it. She asked if I thought it would be beneficial, I said a quick "yes." So she picked up the discussion guide and we started going through the questions.

On the surface the chapter didn't have a lot to do with my situation, but as I was about to find out God can use anything to reach us where we are when we give Him an opportunity.

It started with a quote from the book,

> *"Why assume the worst? As followers of God, you and I have a huge asset. We know everything is going to turn out all right."*[10]

After reading the quote my friend gave me a knowing glance and repeated, "We know everything is going to turn out all right." I nodded, knowing it on one level, but not believing it on another.

The next question asked us to list Bible passages that say no disaster is ultimately fatal. As I went on to repeat verses like Romans 8:28 and the "I know I have a plan for you" verse from Jeremiah, I started to realize there was a big gap between what I have always said I believed and the way I was letting myself think about my situation. Still though the darkness remained.

Thank God we have people in our lives to press us on when we're about to give up. While my friend kept reading the questions and looking up the required verses, I was sitting on the couch thinking "what in the world does this have to do with me here today?" God was about to work a miracle.

She looked up the next verse and as she read it silently to herself, I saw something change in her face. She met my eyes and said said, "I don't think I can read this." I wondered how bad could this verse really be? As she read the verse aloud with tears in her eyes, my eyes filled up too as I realized God was indeed in our midst and He hadn't forgotten about me. The powerful verse went like this,

> "Do not neglect the spiritual gift you received through the prophecy spoken over you when the elders of the church laid their hands on you. Give your complete attention to these matters. Throw yourself into your tasks so that everyone will see your progress. Keep a close watch on how you live and on your teaching. Stay true to what is right for the sake of your own salvation and the salvation of those who hear you." (1 Timothy 4:14-16)

On first glance, this verse might have not had any significance to my situation, but less than an hour before my friend had been trying to encourage me to hold fast, not give up and keep serving God because He had a big plan for me and I was going to make a big impact for the Kingdom. She believed if I stood my ground, God was going to use this situation to prepare me and my gifts to reach the world for Him. My pastor had echoed those same thoughts just days before when we met in his office. Me being me I didn't believe either of them, but after reading the verses I realized that God was speaking. And He wasn't done.

After regaining our composure, we were floored when we realized she had "accidentally" gone to 1 Timothy when the discussion guide wanted us to read from 2 Timothy. The verse from 2 Timothy was just as pertinent as the "mistaken" one:

> "And I was delivered from the lion's mouth.
> The Lord will rescue me from every evil attack
> and will bring me safely to His heavenly kingdom."
> (2 Timothy 4:17-18, NIV)

By this point we both had tears in our eyes again and were pretty speechless at the way God was speaking to me through a chapter and discussion guide which at first had seemingly nothing to do with my circumstances.

We started praying and I felt the presence of God come down an encompassing way. The tears were flowing and this time around they were for a good reason. As we prayed I felt the darkness lifting from my soul and the light of Christ was filling every crack and crevice.

When my mom saw me afterwards she could see the difference written all over my face. Once darkness was my constant companion; now light came back into my eyes and onto my face.

Does this mean life suddenly went back to being perfect? Certainly not. In many ways, my darkest days were still ahead of me. But there was a difference in the darkness this time. The difference was I knew that no matter how I felt or no matter how things looked, I was not alone.

The love of God is so strong that it reaches us wherever we are in life — whether in the depth of a depression or on the peak of a mountaintop. God reaches out and takes our hand where we are and leads us through not only the best of times, but the worst of times too.

It was the Apostle Paul who wrote,

> "And I am convinced that nothing can ever separate us
> from God's love. Neither death nor life, neither angels

> *nor demons, neither our fears for today nor our worries about tomorrow — not even the powers of hell can separate us from God's love." (Romans 8:38)*

Satan would have us believe that as soon as life gets hard or the darkness starts to creep in, God has checked out. That couldn't be further from the truth. In the darkest moment of our history, the death of Jesus Christ, to the outside world it might have looked like God had abandoned this carpenter from Nazareth. In the Grand Scheme of things, His story was only getting started. The darkest moment of the cross preceded the dawn of the resurrection which would not only change the course of history, but the lives of everyone who believes.

If our beliefs abandon or change the moment our lives are challenged, we are no better than a bottle bobbing on the ocean that has surrendered itself to the course of the waves. However, if we allow our minds to stay centered on the truth of who we know God to be when the waves start crashing, then we become like the buoy. Our lives might rock with the waves, but we stay anchored where we should be.

The truth of the matter is if Satan can't tear us down with the weight of our circumstances, he doesn't give up. In fact often the greatest spiritual attacks come just before the dawn in our lives. It seems he takes out the calvary and throws everything he can in our path in one last ditch effort to tear us down. Satan tries so hard to keep our eyes clouded by pain because he knows if we could see God clearly even in our pain and darkness, nothing else could ever stand in our way.

Needless to say I stopped taking the medication and once it had worked its way out of my system the depression passed, but the fight for my soul and life was not over. In many ways it had only just begun.

Although when the next wave of the battle came, there was a difference. Before I hit the depression I was like that bottle on the ocean, drifting in the waves of life. However my time in the darkness prepared me for this next challenge. Where even weeks before I would have written off the significance of these events; I recognized them for what they were this time around — all part of a greater plan. And I for one was not going to let Satan take me out at the knees.

We can stop Satan, but we have to choose to stand up. If we allow ourselves to remain complacent and we remove the anchor that Christ is from our lives, we don't stand a chance. When we do keep our eyes open we're told we can stand against him,

> *"Stay alert! Watch out for your great enemy, the devil. He prowls around like a roaring lion, looking for someone to devour. Stand firm against him, and be strong in your faith. Remember that your Christian brothers and sisters all over the world are going through the same kind of suffering you are." (1 Peter 5:8-9)*

Above all, we also need to recognize we aren't in this battle alone. 2 Thessalonians 3:3 teaches us,

> *"But the Lord is faithful; He will strengthen you and guard you from the evil one." (2 Thessalonians 3:3)*

It might seem like the darkness is overwhelming, but we have the light of Christ on our side. That might not always mean we are never exposed to the nighttime of our lives or the dark nights of the soul, but it does mean that even in that place we can know that we are not alone. It also means that even in the darkest place we can hold onto the truth that often it's darkest right before the dawn.

THE DARKNESS BEFORE THE DAWN

Your circumstances might look pitch black. Your faith might be shaken. You might be tired and weary. Despite that, this is no time to give up. Instead it's a time to stand up and fight, holding your ground, knowing this season of darkness might very well also be the season of greatest victory in your life.

CHAPTER TWELVE

Finding Healing at the Wall

"When we become aware that we do not have to escape our pains, but that we can mobilize them into a common search for life, those very pains are transformed from expressions of despair into signs of hope."
— HENRI NOUWEN

Most of my fondest childhood memories surround holidays we used to take with my grandparents. On one particular holiday we jammed, and I mean jammed, three kids and three adults into a rented Buick car and drove ten hours to arrive at our destination in Ottawa, Ontario. The trip kicked off with us on the side of the road, stuffing our jackets into the trunk in an desperate attempt to provide each person with more space. Just moments later we were frantic when Mom attempted to start up the car again and realized the car keys were likely in said trunk. Eventually the keys were found, but our experiences only went downhill from there. Literally.

At one point we found ourselves lost in the city and driving the wrong way down a one way street, with no idea how to get back to our hotel. Or even on the right side of the road for that matter. In desperation my mom pulled off the road, stopped the car at the top of a hill and leapt out of the vehicle to go talk to a police officer she had spotted patrolling the sidewalk. She was hoping he could offer some directions. Unfortunately in her haste to talk to the officer, my mom forgot to do something very important, she didn't put the car in park.

So here we are, three children under the age of 13 squashed in the backseat and two seniors pressed tightly against each other in the front, trapped in this vehicle that is now rolling down a hill. Meanwhile my mom and the police officer are talking away, completely oblivious to our plight.

My grandparents, who were locked into place by their seat belts, tried desperately to put the car in park but couldn't reach the gearshift. My siblings and I looked out the back window and noticed something terrifying: we were on a collision course with a large brick wall at the bottom which was getting closer by the second. Desperate times called for desperate measures so we launched my brother from the backseat headfirst into the driver's seat. With his legs sticking up in the air and his head and hands by the pedals, he managed to hit the brakes and stop the car before we made a permanent impression on the City of Ottawa.

For years we laughed about this incident and refused to let my Mom live it down. Although I'm still laughing there is something profound this incident has taught me.

You see there were two completely different viewpoints shared by those on the scene that day. There were the terrified passengers in the car who would have done anything to avoid crashing into the wall. Then there were those who were unsuspecting that just meters away something terrible was about to happen.

Sadly when it comes to "hitting the wall" in our lives there are those same two schools of thought we can find ourselves in.

Some people can see the wall approaching and they do whatever it takes to hit the brakes.

Others are completely oblivious to its approach. But you know what is interesting? It hits them nonetheless.

So what is the wall? The concept isn't a new one. Some, like Saint John of the Cross and Saint Francis of Assisi, have referred to it as the "dark night of the soul." It's meant to describe a time in a Christian's life when they experience a profound spiritual crisis triggered by a disappointment or a door that closes. Peter Scazzerio defined it as "the Wall" in his incredible book *Emotionally Healthy Spirituality,*

> *"For most of us the Wall appears through a crisis that turns our world upside down. It comes, perhaps, through a divorce, a job loss, the death of a close friend or family member, a cancer diagnosis, a disillusioning church experience, a betrayal, a shattered dream, a wayward child, a car accident, an inability to get pregnant, a deep desire to marry that remains unfulfilled, a dryness or loss of joy in our relationship with God. We question ourselves, God, the church. We discover for the first time that our faith does not appear to "work". We have more questions than answers as the very foundation of our faith feels like it is on the line. We don't know where God is, what He is doing, where He is going, how He is getting there, or when this will be over."*[11]

Have you ever felt like you hit the wall? Or maybe you might be there now? It's a place where the questions you have about your circumstances can't be answered. You feel like you were in over your head, drowning, and you can't see a lifeboat coming your way.

It's not a very pleasant feeling, is it?

In fact "hitting the wall" is so unpleasant many people consciously or subconsciously make themselves oblivious to it. They feel the pain, they have the questions, but instead of acknowledging it and following it where it leads, they hide. They laugh, they make themselves busy, they buy things. They pretty much do whatever it takes to stuff those feelings, questions and doubts into their distant memory and they will do whatever it takes to avoid opening Pandora's Box.

I can say that with reasonable certainty because I was one of those people.

Problems would come and I'd suddenly find myself out the door to the movies.

Questions would plague me and catch phrases would spring up in my mind.

Issues would arise and my eye would find something shiny to buy.

But then the most wonderful terrible thing happened to me (and yes, you read it right). Shortly after my depression experience was in the rearview mirror I found myself in a place where I couldn't run anymore.

Previously it didn't matter how bad things were with my health, everything else seemed to stay held together. Suddenly that was no longer the case. Due to an accumulation of medical bills my finances took a nose dive and at the same time the student loan department came calling, wanting their money back — money I couldn't come up with no matter how hard I tried.

One of my jobs, which had been stable for as far back as I could remember, was no longer stable and I couldn't count on that income to help sustain me anymore as the company was undergoing financial difficulties. As a result, my future with them was no longer a sure thing.

My Chronic Fatigue Syndrome, which was never great, went from bad to worse. I went through a period of time when I had no endurance left. My days were spent moving from the couch to the computer to do what work I could, then back to the couch again. All while suddenly battling widespread pain throughout my body.

And if that wasn't enough one of my closest relationships suddenly went from being stable to very turbulent.

All of this happened within a very short timeframe, which left my head spinning and me wondering why I was being faced with such an onslaught. Even outside observers were wondering the same thing. I'll never forget being prayed over and one person uttered exactly what I was feeling, "God I'm not trying to be rude here, but enough is enough!"

After some thought, one observation I did make at the time is all of these situations had something in common. With some problems there is a visible solution that we can work out and there are things we can do to help improve the situation. However in what I was facing it seemed like my hands were literally tied behind my back.

With my health, I had tried everything there was to try. I had seen all of the doctors; I had taken all of the pills. All I could do was rest and hope this phase would pass.

Regarding my finances, I had stopped spending on anything that wasn't vital some time ago. Unfortunately with all the medical expenses I had there was no quick fix to getting out of debt while paying for the things I needed to make it by in that moment in time.

As to one of my jobs, there was nothing I could do but wait for a decision to be made by someone else over whether or not they could afford to keep me on.

And with my relationship, the ball was literally in the other person's court. Don't get me wrong, I did what I could to handle the hurt with grace and made it clear I had left the door open for reconciliation. But as I was advised, in situations like these there is little one can do but work through the forgiveness process and pray for change.

I am a planner and being locked in a place with no plan to make other than surrender might as well have been torture. Thankfully as I was about to find out, it was the best place in the world I could have been. Why? Because I literally ran headfirst into the wall and there was no quick escape this time.

Having no escape meant that I was going to have to stop running and deal with everything and I mean everything.

Living in the broken world we do, our lives can be quite messy and as Christians we spend a lot of time talking about our spiritual health. Meanwhile as I learned in *Emotionally Healthy Spirituality*, sometimes we're so focused on our spiritual health we end up leaving our emotional health a mess. Furthermore our emotional health, just like our physical health, effects nearly everything we do.

After reading that book, which I highly recommend, I realized that even though I had hit the wall God hadn't left me at the wall alone. His hand was there and He was gently leading me through these land mines, knowing the benefit to my soul outweighed the pain of those moments.

Hitting the wall was perhaps the best thing that could have ever happened to me. I recognized that. I also realized I didn't want to leave that place only partially changed. If God had led me there to do some renovations on my heart, I didn't want to stand in the way of His work so I made a very conscious decision — I decided that no matter the cost, I was going to face the pain head on. I wasn't going to hide from it; I wasn't going to run from it; I was going to let myself feel it and feel it fully.

To someone watching on the outside the results weren't pretty. But through hours of prayer, reading and counseling I was able to sort through the trash in my life which came to the surface with the pain and something beautiful started rising up within me. For the first time in a long time I started to feel and feel deeply. While my body was still asleep, my soul awakened and came alive in a way that I could have never planned or can even explain. In many ways I experienced exactly what Henri Nouwen described,

> *"It is important that you dare to stay with your pain and allow it to be there. The pain you suffer now is meant to put you in touch with the place where you need healing, your very heart. Dare to stay with your pain and trust in God's promise to you."* [12]

Isn't that a precious thought? The pain we suffer right here and now has purpose because it puts us in touch with the places we need healing — namely our hearts.

Pain works like an MRI; it gives us a clear picture of exactly what is wrong in our lives and our hearts. When life is good we can cover up the condition of our hearts with such things as success, status, relationships and our bank accounts. When pain comes, on the other hand, it takes away our picture of perfection and reveals what's really going on under the surface. Our past hurts surface, the real status of our relationships get revealed and our hearts stop playing games and start crying out for healing in the places we've really been hurting all along.

When this happens we give God the kind of canvas He can really work on. When we come to Him humbled by our brokenness, we find something more valuable than anything else — we find healing. The Bible comforts us,

> *"[God] heals the brokenhearted and bandages their wounds." (Psalm 147:3)*

He clearly says,

> *"As the clay is in the potter's hand, so are you in My hand." (Jeremiah 18:6)*

God goes to work on our heart as only He can and something inside of us changes. The pieces of our heart start to be put back together. Gradually we feel more, we connect with Him more, and we start to feel more alive. The very hearts that were dulled become sharp again and return to us the wonder, awe, and love we had lost long ago. In many ways we become like children and when we do, we realize being child-like before God is a strength, not a weakness.

Pain takes away the pretenses we allowed ourselves to hide behind for way too long and turns us into authentic people. People who can admit they are broken, but don't leave it at that. Their very lives and their very brokenness points those around them to the Healer.

The pain isn't easy, but by allowing ourselves to feel it, we allow it to serve its purpose in refining us,

> *"Dear brothers and sisters, when troubles of any kind come your way, consider it an opportunity for great joy. For you know that when your faith is tested, your endurance has a chance to grow. So let it grow, for when your endurance is fully developed, you will be perfect and complete, needing nothing." (James 1:2-4)*

There is no short cut to growth. No magic pill we can take which instantly heals our hearts and transforms us. Knowing that, we should take a different approach at how we view those instances in our lives with no quick fix or sudden solution. Rather than viewing them as the worst possible situations that could have unfolded, we should view them as an opportunity for growth. Instead of looking for a quick escape route we should allow ourselves to be brought down on our knees at the wall and then wait there, with open hearts and minds, ready for God to do a great work in our lives.

The choice is with us though. We could be like my brother, diving over any obstacle to avoid hitting the wall. We could be like my mother and the police officer, oblivious to the oncoming disaster. Or we could be like Job, a man who put his life on pause to deal with the questions, the doubt and the pain. Job hit the wall and he refused to leave until the pain was dealt with. After being in all three scenarios I can tell you that while this route is at first glance the more painful one, it is the only one which leads to a beautiful Redemption story in the end.

Truthfully God does write a story of Redemption in each of our lives. It unfolds as we walk with Him on this earth and leads to a spectacular grande finale when we cross the finish line from this life and into the next.

CHAPTER THIRTEEN

Waiting for Sunday

"The best we can hope for in this life is a knothole peek at the shining realities ahead. Yet a glimpse is enough. It's enough to convince our hearts that whatever sufferings and sorrows currently assail us aren't worthy of comparison to that which waits over the horizon."
— JONI EARECKSON TADA

A few years ago my church brought a production into town called "Fish Eyes." The basic premise of the story was following the lives of Peter and Andrew, brothers who also were disciples of Jesus.

Even though I previously read and heard the stories which were portrayed on the stage many times before, something about seeing it acted out right before me brought those ancient words to life once again. It wasn't because of fancy special effects. In fact the entire production consisted of two actors on a stage with a backdrop and three coolers. What made this production so powerful was the acting. Seeing firsthand the expressions, body language and tone of voice that portrayed what the disciples might have been thinking and feeling during their time with Jesus.

One of the parts of the production that struck me the most was Peter and Andrew's reaction when Jesus was arrested. From the looks on the actors faces you could see the deep despair and heartbreak they felt. It was something I never gave a lot of thought to before, but it's an essential part of the story. Let's just think about it for a minute.

Here is a group of 12 guys who literally left everything they had and everyone they loved to follow Christ. They joined Him for a three and a half year time period in which they really bonded with Him. He was their Best Friend, the one whom they loved with everything they had and trusted Him with all of their beings. With Him they were turned from ordinary men and outcasts into beloved friends and trusted ministry partners. Jesus didn't treat them as though they were inferior; on the contrary, He treated them like they were His brothers and partners on the journey.

Palm Sunday rolls around and as the disciples parade through the streets with Jesus, you could imagine their elation and exuberant joy. Walking through a crowd roaring at the sight of this Man would be like crowd surfing with Bono at a U2 concert; running onto center field after your favorite team wins the Super Bowl; or doing a victory lap with a cyclist who just crossed the finish line after winning the Tour de France. It would be a moment of elation as you're identified with the celebrity of the moment and you're surfing their wave of popularity with them.

After a scene like this, could you imagine the kind of spiritual high these disciples must have been on? Their purpose was probably never so clear, their resolve to follow Christ never so secure. Finally everyone else was seeing what they saw in Jesus and maybe, just maybe, this whole ministry thing was going to get a little easier.

Fast forward a few days and the climate completely changes. Their beloved Leader has been arrested. Days ago being associated with Jesus was a valuable commodity, but they now had some serious incentive (namely death or torture) to put some distance there. The adoring crowds were replaced with angry ones. And the twelve men who had bonded together over the past three years scattered in whichever direction led them a safe distance away from the controversy and criminal proceedings.

They were high one minute, cast into the ultimate low the next. It's little wonder why in Fish Eyes, the actors choose to show such agony and despair on the faces of the two disciples in the production. In the time it took for Judas to greet Jesus with a kiss, sealing the act of betrayal, their hopes, dreams and futures were completely derailed.

Jesus was sentenced to death and while I'm sure they thought He was going to perform some sort of miraculous deliverance, they were forced to stand at a distance and watch their Leader die. As Jesus drew His last breath, their hopes for a last minute "hail Mary" in the story were crushed. Jesus was gone and with Him went their dreams and their futures. Or so they thought.

While we cannot know exactly what kind of thoughts were running through their minds after Jesus' brutal death, I can only imagine there was a deep sense of doubt there.

"Were we wrong about Jesus?"

"Was He just like every other prophet or good teacher?"

"Who was I to ever think I could be more than a fisherman?"

We're told in the Gospels that some of the disciples made the painful journey back to their own lives and old professions after Jesus was crucified. Peter and his friends went from casting out demons to casting out their fishing nets and even at that they weren't successful anymore.

They were trapped between Good Friday and Easter Sunday — between the death and the resurrection, between the despair and the joy.

Maybe you can relate because it's the same place you've found yourself in. A door has closed and you've seen your dreams placed into a coffin and lowered into the grave. Now you're standing there, empty handed and not knowing where to go from here.

As hard as it may be to hear this, we need to realize that in many ways we have it easier than the disciples did. Why? Because they had no idea their Easter Sunday was coming. When we celebrate Good Friday in church we feel sadness, but also hope as we are reminded that Easter Sunday is coming. The disciples didn't have the benefit of this knowledge. When they left Calvary on that dark day, they thought this was the end of the road. They didn't realize that just two days later their worlds would be forever changed when Jesus would rise from the dead and re-appear.

We see the depth of their Good Friday despair clearly illustrated in Thomas' reaction to the news that Jesus was risen from the dead. Instead of rejoicing that his friend was alive, Thomas was so dejected and likely depressed over what happened at Calvary he could not account for the possibility of another chapter in the story,

> "[The other disciples] told him, 'We have seen the Lord!' But [Thomas] replied, 'I won't believe it unless I see the nail wounds in His hands, put my fingers into them, and place my hand into the wound in his side."
> (John 20:25)

God was just getting started, but Thomas had already written "The End" in bold print and he wasn't in any hurry to change it.

Maybe you can relate to Thomas because you've experienced your own version of a Good Friday in your life. In this place you can't picture the possibility of a resurrection.

Your spouse walked out the door and you've buried your marriage and the hope of love alongside it.

Your boss handed you a pink slip and down went your dream job in flames, burned beyond recognition.

An illness has hung around for far too long and besides stealing your health, it's taken too much of your time, money, and plans for the future.

It's a bleak forecast for your life and no matter how hard you try to see beyond the storm clouds, you can't bring yourself to hope there could ever be the chance of sunshine in this area of your life again.

Many times in our lives we will be stuck in a place between a crucifixion and resurrection — a death and a birthing of new life. For the disciples that period of time was a mere few days. For our life stories, we can be stuck in the waiting room for much longer.

So where does that leave us during these waiting room times in life? Well, it leaves us with a choice. If you've ever spent much time in an actual waiting room, you know there are different characters who surface in those crowded rooms.

There's usually the Exasperated. The one person who can't believe they are being asked to wait for even a few moments. They can't sit still. They can't enjoy a minute of silence. They can't even pick up a magazine. They are so focused on the minutes spent in waiting that they make the waiting room a completely miserable place to be for both themselves and anyone within earshot.

Sometimes sitting next to the Exasperated is the Cool and Collected. He is the guy who's reading that magazine with such interest you would swear each article was custom written for him. When his name is finally called, he answers with a smile and a pause as he returns the magazine neatly on the rack as if an hour or two hadn't passed him by in this waiting room.

Then over there in the corner is Mr. CEO with the smartphone. Dressed professionally, he is usually polite about the wait, but at the same time wants everyone in that waiting room to realize just how important he is. He pounds on his little keyboard with his thumbs like the world will go down in flames if he looks away from it for merely a minute.

Same wait, different people, with very different reactions to their circumstances.

No matter what your natural tendency is during your wait times in life, we all need to realize there is a value to be found in waiting. Not only does it refine our character by increasing our patience, but it provides us with something that our fast paced society rarely does — time.

We are very busy people, usually on the go. When we're put in a waiting room in our life, whether it's a time between jobs or a time between knowing what was and what might come next, we're given the rare opportunity to stop and actually be still. That's very rare in our world, but it is a valuable experience to embrace.

Many of us are scared to embrace the wait times because we're afraid if we sit still too long either we'll either never get back in the game, people will think something badly of us for our pause or we'll be forced to spend time with ourselves and maybe not like the person we discover. Whatever your hesitation, know this; waiting isn't easy, but it is vital.

In Isaiah 40, we're taught it's by waiting that we gain strength,

> *"But they that wait upon the Lord shall renew their strength; they shall mount up with wings as eagles; they shall run, and not be weary; and they shall walk, and not faint." (Isaiah 40:31)* [13]

Do you see that? By waiting we are strengthened. Not by keeping busy and certainly not by being productive, but by waiting.

During these times of waiting it's very important for us to not only allow ourselves to be shaped by God, but to realize that although the outlook is bleak, we don't know the whole story. Until we do, we should never give up hope. Sometimes it may look like our resurrection moment will never come or the probability of it happening is nil. That's no reason to give up. As the people of England in the 1800's found out, sometimes things are not as they seem.

In June 1815 the story is told that the people of England were impatiently waiting to hear what was happening at the Battle of Waterloo in Belgium. Their army, under the command of the Duke of Wellington, was fighting against the French army led by the feared Napoleon Bonaparte.

In order to get word from the battlefield to the streets of England, the British set up a series of communication points. Each point was in sight of the other and signals were used to relay messages from the frontline. After waiting on pins and needles, finally a message started to work its way down the communication line. The message? "Wellington defeated."

To the people of England, this was the worst news imaginable. Their strong army led by their brave commander had been defeated. Not only would Napoleon be given further opportunity to advance, but their very country was in jeopardy.

If you were living in England in 1815 and you heard the heartbreaking message, chances are you'd be filled with fear and despair. Would anyone really blame you for being in that state? Maybe you had a son, a brother or a father on the battlefield whose blood had most likely been spilled in vain. And let's face it, the outlook for your country and thus your safety just became very bleak.

Ironically while the people of England were sinking into a depression, the battlefield at Waterloo was filled with celebration. The real truth was although it was not visible from England, the British army had indeed been victorious. The reason for the miscommunication? A fog bank had rolled in and blocked the signals, cutting off the message. "Wellington defeated" really should have read "Wellington defeated Napoleon at Waterloo."

The people of England didn't know the whole story and thus, they were blinded to reality. Instead of celebrating the end of Napoleon's quest to conquer Europe, they were depressed and worried about the future.

I wonder how often do we miss the whole message? The fog rolls into our lives and we start missing the whole picture. It might look like a dead end in our eyes, but maybe it looks that way because we are blinded to what's coming down the road in front of us. Maybe the place we'll travel to next is not much different in landscape, but will hold the answers to some of our questions and will bring understanding.

So maybe instead of pacing in our own version of life's waiting room, we should instead learn to be still before God. Victory might be a lot closer than we think.

CHAPTER FOURTEEN

Waking Up in Babylon

"It is true that God may have called you to be exactly where you are. But, it is absolutely vital to grasp that He didn't call you there so you could settle in and live your life in comfort and superficial peace."
— FRANCIS CHAN

Ezekiel is one person whose story was told in the Bible who was familiar with closed doors. I know that Ezekiel's story isn't one that many of us spend a whole lot of time dwelling on. You probably, like me, find that book in the Bible an easy one to skip over because of all the obscure imagery which is hard to understand and is mixed in with messages of judgment. It is, however, an important one to read and understand especially when facing a closed door.

Ezekiel, who for the purposes of better storytelling, I'm going to call Zeke. Why? Because when I hear the name Ezekiel I picture someone older (my apologies to any younger person with this beautiful name). So for the sake of being able to picture his story a little better, I'm going to call him Zeke.

Zeke was born into a priesthood family. This meant his dad was a priest, serving in God's temple in Jerusalem and soon Zeke would be following in his dads footsteps as it was the custom for the priesthood to be passed down from father to son. While many of Zeke's friends were probably tossing around different career options, for Zeke his future had already been laid out. Or so he thought.

When he was only 25 years old, his country was invaded. Zeke was taken in captivity and forced to travel over 700 miles in the desert to a place called Babylon. For Zeke, not only was he leaving his homeland behind, but also his wife (who later tragically dies), his family, his career and his culture. Here is a guy who spent his whole life working towards serving God as a priest, but he still loses everything that is familiar.

When we encounter him in Ezekiel chapter one, we pick up the story five years after he was first forced out of his homeland and made to live as a foreigner amongst people who did not follow, serve or believe in the same God he did. At this point Zeke is thirty years of age. This might not seem like a significant age to you or I, but for Zeke the minute he blew out the candles on the cake on his thirtieth birthday it meant he was ready to stop preparing and actually become a priest. According to Jewish culture men would not become priests until they turned 30 (see Numbers 4:30). Celebrating his birthday that year had to have been bittersweet for Zeke. Everything he had spent a lifetime preparing for was out of reach because Zeke wasn't in Jerusalem anymore and outside of Jerusalem, where the temple was found, there weren't a lot of want ads asking for priests.

If anyone could recognize a slamming door, it was Zeke.

I don't know whether or not Zeke spent a significant amount of time questioning the change in his life's course or if he faced his own version of the dark night of the soul during his first five years in Babylon. What I do know is Zeke followed in the footsteps of Daniel and found that sometimes a God-given destiny can be found even when you are in exile.

Instead of living the life he was groomed for as a priest in Jerusalem, Zeke lived the life God groomed him for in exile — a prophet in a land where his voice was one of few, if any, calling people back to God. While this wasn't a planned destination when

Zeke was drawing out the map of his life, he went with the map God had drawn instead. As a result he became one of the most influential prophets of all time. A prophet who, in his own words, saw visions of God,

> *"On July 31 of my thirtieth year, while I was with the Judean exiles beside the Kebar River in Babylon, the heavens were opened and I saw visions of God. This happened during the fifth year of King Jehoiachin's captivity. (The Lord gave this message to Ezekiel son of Buzi, a priest, beside the Kebar River in the land of the Babylonians, and he felt the hand of the Lord take hold of him.)" (Ezekiel 1:1-3)*

God used Zeke to speak to his neighbors in Babylon thousands of years ago and God's plans for Zeke didn't stop there. His words have impacted generations upon generations and his story still serves as an inspiration to you and I today. Through Zeke we learn the life God has planned for us far outweighs anything we could ever dream or prepare for on our own. Through his story we are also reminded how sometimes God needs to bring us away from everything we cherish in order to show us that what we've been hanging onto is worthless. And maybe, just maybe, God allows us to be pulled away from anything familiar so that we can see that in Him we have the only sense of home we really need.

While we aren't given the exact details of Zeke's journey of accepting his new God-given role, we do know a journey would have had to of taken place. Zeke would have had to come to the place where he surrendered his plans of priesthood in Jerusalem or he would have never been equipped or ready to accept God's plan of being a prophet in Babylon.

This is important to realize because it's something both you and I both do when we face closed doors and find ourselves asking

"How in the world did I get here?" or "Why did this happen to me?". While we may never find understanding or answers, until we stand ready to surrender our ideas of what today should have look like, we will never be ready for what God has written for our tomorrow.

This isn't an easy place to come to. But it is one where we are following in the footsteps of many people besides Ezekiel.

Abraham built a life in Ur, but at 75 years of age, God called him away from his homeland and onto a new journey.

Moses received his paging from God to a new start when he was 80 years old.

David was summoned to leave life as he knew it as a shepherd in order to face off against a giant that no one else was willing to stand up to. Even after he defeated the giant, David didn't arrive at his destination as King of Israel right away. Instead he spent a good deal of time on the run, fearing for his life.

These days I can really relate with those Biblical heroes.

You know my story about how after I had what was supposed to be a routine surgery, I ended up with an infection which took six long months to heal. Afterwards instead of returning to good health, I was forced to walk the road of life in the shoes of someone who had Chronic Fatigue Syndrome and major sleep issues. Nearly every day I looked for the end to come into sight. I thought that day came when I tried the "miracle medication" only to be disappointed again. Still in the back of my mind I was longing for the moment when I would wake up feeling refreshed, sleep battles behind me, ready to embrace my Hollywood ending.

And sure enough the day did come.

In March 2011 after having my sleep do another downward spiral I couldn't take it anymore. I was so exhausted I felt physically ill everyday and this feeling of panic started to overtake me as I realized that I no longer had anything left to give. I had used all of my reserves and something was going to have to change because I didn't have it in me to keep going like this.

Imagine my great relief when weeks later I started waking up in the morning with an odd sensation. Or I should say odd lack of sensation. Instead of walking up and feeling like a dump truck ran me sometime during the night, I actually felt nothing — no pain, no exhaustion, no foggy thoughts. There aren't enough exclamation marks in the world to capture just how wonderful it was for me!!!!!!!! I was removed from the desert of chronic disease and while there was no scientific explanation to explain it, I willingly went with it and thanked God profusely for it.

After a couple of months of allowing my body to bounce back I started planning for the future — the one that I was convinced God had written for me. I saved up and bought my first vehicle, a new to me Honda CRV. After months of praying about what path to take for my career I felt strongly that I was supposed to open up my own business. This was confirmed time and time again, so I went through the ropes of writing a business plan, searching out funding and spending as much time as I could getting ready to launch. I took on more commitments as I now had the energy to have a full plate. I joined a young adults small group and saw my life transform through the group as I was encouraged and challenged by some incredible people. Life was good — or at least my definition of good.

This lasted for a year and a half. Right when I was on the verge of launching my business, a business that I had no doubt God did ordained for me, I started noticing something was off. It began with a few bad nights which turned into more than a few. Then came the feeling of memory loss and foggy thoughts, which was soon accompanied by pain. But where before my health problems ended here, this time my body was only getting started. It wasn't long before I was assaulted with all kinds of weird symptoms, including but not limited to, painful growths showing up in weird places on my bones. With the discovery of my right knee being two inches "wider" than it had been just days before I could no longer deny that something was seriously wrong. So I did what I do best — I freaked out and ran to medical professionals looking for help.

Over the next few months I bounced from one doctor to another as my health continued to decline at a rather rapid place. Out of the blue I could no longer keep food down and would have the need to throw up after eating and every day like clockwork at 5 pm and 5 am. Many nights I was forced to spend on the bathroom floor, exhausted and in pain with my throat burned from the acid.

While all of this was happening I had one glimmer of hope on the horizon. One of the members of my health team ordered a test and the results that came back were off. In their opinion that alone could explain most, if not all, of my symptoms. After having a second test to confirm the results were accurate I was sent out of town to a specialist who I was told was the expert to see in this area. After my appointment with him, I was sent to do further testing and was hopeful an answer was going to soon be coming my way.

Then came the phone call. The words pouring out that while he was very sorry for what I was going through, the tests held no answers and he wasn't sure where I should go from there.

Talk about devastating! If being diagnosed with an illness is scary, knowing you have something wrong and no one knows what it is can be terrifying.

At the time that this book is printed I still don't have solid answers. One doctor I saw suggested an auto-immune disease, but weeks later traded in that diagnosis for a muscle-related illness that could explain the pain away, but doesn't explain many of my other symptoms. This fall after my body developed another new symptom, a high heart rate and the feeling of having to pass out just from standing, another doctor determined autonomic dysfunction was likely the root of all my symptoms. And while that does make sense to me, there is still debate among my medical team whether or not that's the case and no solid treatment plan has been presented to treat it.

In the meantime I'm left dealing with symptoms I wouldn't wish on anyone and the assumption this isn't something that will be be solved overnight. As a result, a lot of my plans for the future were bluntly put on hold, leaving me feeling a little cheated.

I mean I had prayed, hadn't I? I had sought out God before I decided to go ahead with different plans and open a business. If He knew this was coming why didn't He give me a holy heads up? Why did He let me go ahead with it?

And that is when His still quiet voice reminded me of something,

"When did I say your business was going to be full-time?"

Check and mate.

I learned something profound that day — something I wish I could have grasped much earlier. Which is I often assume a lot when it comes to God's plans for my life. I envision my life like some sort of Hollywood story, with a defined beginning and end, where everything is neatly wrapped up before the credits roll. In reality our lives often look much differently. They are a little less Hollywood and a little more like those Biblical journeys I've eluded to. That said, maybe instead of hanging onto our ideals we need to change our perspective.

When we look at life with its sole purpose to make us happy by delivering exactly the story we have written for ourselves, we're bound to be disappointed. Even though we all have great seasons and times of bountiful blessings, often those seasons come to us in ways we would have never expected or imagined.

On the other hand when we look at life as an amazing story God has written for us, with twists and turns that carry purpose, we find ourselves caught up in an amazing adventure where we see each detour as just another step in this incredible journey. We are able to embrace that kind of purpose only when we come to really trust in the One who is leading us.

Look at it this way. Imagine if for your birthday this year your friend picked you up after work and blindfolded you (and just for the record, it doesn't take a lot of imagining on my part since this has actually happened to me). After riding for a few minutes blindfolded in the car, chances are you've completely lost your sense of direction and have no idea where you are or where you are going. However you probably aren't going to be freaking out, unless of course you have serious trust issues. Instead of flipping out you're likely excited, wondering where this little journey is going to take you and who is waiting for you on the other end.

Now imagine a different scenario. Instead of your friend picking you up after work and blindfolding you, it is a complete stranger. That would be a reason to not only panic, but to do everything humanly possible to escape, wouldn't it?

That said, the God who is leading our journeys isn't some random stranger with unknown intentions. We know and must keep reminding ourselves it is God who is the One who is leading us down this path. This is the same God who loves us so much He not only forgives us time and time again, but He Himself paid the ultimate sacrifice for that forgiveness. Doesn't that change everything? We don't need to freak out or resist His every move. Instead we can relax and surrender ourselves to His plans, knowing that a friend is the One leading us and He loves us more than we can even imagine.

Knowing I'm being led by a friend rather than a foe makes all the difference for me. As I picture the gentle image of Jesus steering my journey, I'm able to surrender the wheel and even learn to enjoy the journey.

Yes, Zeke's life took a drastic turn from what was expected. Yes, your life might not turn out the way you had planned. And yes, my life looks different right now than I would have thought it would be, but I'm learning the definition of different isn't bad. It's just, well, different.

CHAPTER FIFTEEN

The God Who Goes Before Us

*"The Lord himself goes before you and will be with you;
He will never leave you nor forsake you.
Do not be afraid; do not be discouraged."*
DEUTERONOMY 31:8, NIV

My grandfather was a Canadian solider in the second world war. Growing up we would hear many stories about his time in the army, including the story of how he met my grandmother when he and his friend were looking for a place to stay in Holland after the war was over. They just happened to knock on my grandmother's door and her parents just happened to say "yes" to their request and the rest was history.

One other story has always stuck with me though, the story he told of a night when he was in England.

He went with some of his army buddies to a pub for an evening out when they were on leave. When they entered the pub it was still light outside and the sky was clear; however when they went to leave it was a completely different story. Darkness had fallen and so had the thick pea-soup fog England is known for.

This presented a problem for these Canadians who were in an unknown country, with no idea of how to get back to where they needed to be. The fog was so thick they couldn't tell if they were crossing the street, let alone what direction they were walking in.

When I hear him tell this story I can relate because sadly many times in my own life I feel like I'm wandering in the fog. It seems like I walk into situations when it's sunny outside, only to find myself suddenly plunged into an oppressive fog in an unfamiliar land days, weeks or months later. Leaving me not knowing where to go or what to do.

But the story doesn't end there — at least it didn't for my grandfather in England. In the midst of the fog he saw a dim light and as the light approached, he saw a sight that over 60 years later he would not forget. In the middle of this dangerous fog came a trolley. Needless to say not only was driving in these conditions extremely dangerous, but the fog made it impossible for the driver to navigate. Fortunately, the driver wasn't alone. Instead of traipsing the streets unassisted, the driver had someone in his court who made a world of difference.

Walking ahead of the trolly was a man with two lanterns. Even though the driver could barely see past his own windshield, the man on the ground had enough light to see the road and used his lanterns to guide the driver in the right direction. This lantern holder was no stranger to the streets. He knew them well and while some would become disoriented in the fog, he had the ability to lead others to safety.

Growing up as I heard this story I was always a little envious of the driver who had such a man assisting him. Let me tell you there have been many days, moments and instances when I wished I had someone walking a head to point me in the right direction.

When I didn't know which school to pick.

When I've had to make financial decisions.

When I've needed to choose where to invest my time.

That said, imagine my pleasant surprise when recently God has been bringing a different part of His character to light in my life. Reading through the Bible I've been finding a theme when it comes to who God is and what He does. I've learned through the Bible that the God we follow is not only Lord, Savior, or Jehovah-Jireh, but He is also the God who goes before. This is highlighted in verses in both the Old and New Testament,

> *"The Lord himself goes before you and will be with you; He will never leave you nor forsake you. Do not be afraid; do not be discouraged." (Deuteronomy 31:8, NIV)*

> *"I saw the Lord always before me. Because He is at my right hand, I will not be shaken." (Acts 2:25, NIV)*

> *"I will go before you and will level the mountains; I will break down gates of bronze and cut through bars of iron. I will give you hidden treasures, riches stored in secret places, so that you may know that I am the Lord, the God of Israel, who summons you by name." (Isaiah 45:2-3, NIV)*

Like a shepherd who walks before his flock to make sure the land before them is safe, God walks ahead of His children to scout out the land and lead us in the right direction. It doesn't matter how many unknowns we have on the road ahead of us, He goes before.

We see this in Deuteronomy chapter 9. The Israelites were about to cross into a land with armies and people who were much greater than they were. Facing off in a war against a foe you know is stronger than you is not a good place to be in. It would be like picking a street fight with a professional boxer — not a wise idea unless your idea of a good time is being beaten up pretty badly or even killed.

So the Israelites were facing a very scary situation. They were purposefully walking into a fight they couldn't win on their own, yet they could do so with confidence because they knew one thing — they were following the God who went before.

> *"But be assured today that the Lord your God is the one who goes across ahead of you like a devouring fire. He will destroy them; he will subdue them before you. And you will drive them out and annihilate them quickly, as the Lord has promised you."*
> *(Deuteronomy 9:3, NIV)*

We see this very promise fulfilled as the people of Israel walk in faith behind the God who goes before and He faithfully leads them to victory.

So what land are you needing to cross into? Maybe after years of closed doors you can finally see one opening but are afraid to walk through it. You need to know no matter what lies ahead, you can walk in with confidence knowing you follow the God who goes before.

He goes before you into the job interview.

He goes before you into the courtroom.

He goes before you into the church meeting.

He goes before you into the coffee shop.

No matter where you find yourself in life, you're following the footsteps of someone who walks ahead. It's similar to what would happen when I was a child and we'd go to scout out the perfect Christmas tree. We'd make our way through deep snow to find a tree, often in an area which was very unfamiliar. But it was never a cause for concern though for two reasons. First off, we were following my Mom who knew where she was going and secondly we were walking in her very footsteps. Instead of breaking our own trail and growing weary and tired in the process, we were stepping exactly where she had once stood, confirming we were on the right path and easing the load.

The same goes for you and I as we journey through our lives. We are not breaking our own trail, rather we're following in the footsteps of the very Man who lived on earth Himself for 33 years; He knows exactly what it is like. Jesus didn't have to stay on earth for 33 years in order to accomplish His purpose of salvation. He could have given His life at age 12 or 16 or 21. Rather He choose to hang around for many more years; maybe the reason being so He would know what it's like and He'd be equipped to lead the way.

It doesn't matter how many doors have closed in the past, how thick the fog is now or how lost you feel, you need to remember you are not alone! God is with you and as long as you follow Him step by step, like the man with the lanterns, He'll lead you safely to your destination.

This territory of your life that may seem so foreign to you is known by God inside out. He's not leading you in this direction by chance. He sees what's beyond the fog, He's leading you down roads which are not only going to take you to exactly where you need to be, but are also going to make you the kind of person He desires as you journey.

You are not alone. You are following the God who goes before.

CHAPTER SIXTEEN

The Last Chapter of the Book, Not Your Life Story

"Sometimes it is the destinations out of reach that create the circumstances God uses to remind us that we are never out of His reach."

— ANDY STANLEY

For months my Mom has been asking me the same question week after week. What was her question? "So have you finished the book yet?" And the answer was always the same, "No."

No matter how many hours I spent writing and how much I thought, studied and prayed, I couldn't call the book done. It just seemed something was missing.

Thankfully I figured out what that something was.

You see every book has a conclusion to it, but I couldn't come up with one. Maybe I was falling into the self-help trap and hoping to find a few magical steps you and I could do to wrap up our time in the in between a closed door and an open one. Maybe I was trying to come up with some profound way to explain away the mystery which can surround these periods in our lives. But I think a bigger part of it is I was waiting for the time of facing closed doors to be over in my own life so I could write from the other side of it. I wanted to encourage you and I that if we keep pressing on, one day there will be this divine revelation and magical "ah ha!" moment when everything is clear and life is smooth sailing with nothing but open doors from there on out.

But I've come to realize that while some of us might enjoy those moments for periods in our lives, most of us spend large portions of our lives in waiting rooms of life and valleys and deserts. I've also come to realize maybe it's in those places that real living is meant to take place.

After all, for all the time he walked on this earth, Moses spent not one day of his life in the Promised Land.

David might have been pointed out as a future King at a young age, but he waited some time before the crown arrived. And even when it did, more time was spent in battles and running for his life than was spent in the comfort of a castle.

And Jesus might have had just over three incredible years of public ministry, but the rest of his life on this earth remains a mystery to us. Let's not forget even his public ministry also included a brutal death.

Sometimes what we view as the detour really is the destination. More often than not we only find this out in hindsight.

Isn't that the story of our lives? Most of the time the pictures of our lives are clearer looking in the rearview mirror than they are out the front windshield.

Knowing this, the only "conclusion" or "send off" I could leave you with is the same one I've learned to hang onto myself — don't judge this chapter in your story, instead embrace it.

If the God of the Universe has placed you here, embrace it, welcome it and live out everyday to the fullest. If one day He calls you to come out of this wilderness, then by all means go. In the meantime though, don't make the same mistake I have in the past in labeling this part of our lives as something less significant than what is to come. Yes, God may have great things for us around the corner, but because our perspective is limited, how can we judge that the here and now isn't something marvelous as well? It may not look like it at the moment but it very well may be.

Often in hindsight we can see those very moments we would have hit "Fast Forward" or "Skip Scene" on, are really the moments that define us as individuals, refine us as followers of Christ and can turn the world as we know it upside down. God can create beauty out of the ashes.

Such is the story of my favorite city.

I visited Chicago for the first time in 2008 and to say it was fabulous is an understatement. Seeing firsthand the landscape I'd seen in movies, read about in books, and researched for years was an incredible experience. It wasn't long, however, before I found out that what makes Chicago, well Chicago, isn't its moments of triumph but rather what the people of Chicago did after its near destruction.

In October of 1871 a great fire spread throughout a good part of the city and burned almost everything in its path. As a result many of the landmarks were destroyed and over 100,000 people were left homeless. Instead of packing up and moving on to another city, the people and officials of Chicago dug their heals in and decided to rebuild.

The result is the City of Chicago as we know it today.

They took the ashes and debris from the fire and dumped it along the waterfront, which created the land which attractions like Grant Park and Soldier Field are housed on. This land remains free and open to the public, protected from developers snatching it up. It has resulted in a waterfront unlike any other I've seen.

Rather than constructing duplicates of the buildings that were lost in an effort to recreate the past they embraced the future. Architects from around the world flocked to Chicago and helped to create the magnificent and unique skyline people still awe over today.

Chicago could have turned into a desolate city as a result of the fire. On the contrary it turned into something stronger and something greater. Chicago literally rose out of the ashes with character, beauty, and purpose. Over a hundred and forty years later that purpose is not lost on its residents. Unlike the residents of many other large cities, the people of Chicago love showing you their city. They love telling the story of how it rose from the ashes; they love the character which makes their city theirs.

When you visit Chicago today you don't see ashes; you see beauty. It might not have looked like it in 1871, but the city today tells a story of redemption that only the perspective of time can tell.

The same can be true in our lives.

You might never understand why you're going through what you're going through now. You might never get a real reason why you had to wander in the desert during your days here on earth or why it seems like you're faced with nothing but slamming doors. But please, whatever you do, don't let a lack of answers be your story.

Let your story be one of a life that is so committed to following Jesus and so focused on Him that no matter what happens, your life glorifies Him. Instead of sitting in the ashes and remaining there until you get answers, put your trust in God and follow where He leads. Let Him take the flames and use them to refine you and your life story into gold.

When you let your life be not about "why?" but about "what should you have me do, Lord?" the result is a beautiful portrait of redemption and grace.

On this journey you're going to find that He can do incredible things even in circumstances that don't make sense to you. The fact that you are reading this book is one example of that. Not one word was written while I was in a place that I planned on being in or would have ever wanted to find myself in. But even in those unplanned circumstances I found out something I wouldn't trade for anything — the knowledge that His plans are so much better!

So put away the map.

Stop trying to program the GPS of your life.

Instead keep your eyes on Jesus.

He calls us to follow Him and when we say "Yes Lord" He leads. You may not see where you're going, but the beauty is you don't need to because you're following the One who built the road and knows it better than we could ever.

When you live your life this way, something remarkable happens. The circumstances might not change, but we do. We are filled with peace, guided by wisdom and equipped to live each day abundantly.

So what about you?

Are you going to give up the quest for control and instead find peace in surrender?

Are you going to choose to walk the road of fear, resentment, worry and discontentment? Or are you going to walk the path of trust, love, faith and purpose?

I know which path I'm choosing. The question I wanted to conclude with is, "Will you be joining me on this journey?" It's my heartfelt prayer you do.

Bibliography

[1] Dietrich Bonhoeffer, *The Cost of Discipleship*, Touchstone, September 1, 1995, p. 58

[2] Hebrews 11, *The Message: The Bible In Contemporary Language*, Eugene H. Peterson, NavPress, September 8, 2005

[3] Erich Fromm, *1968: The Revolution of Hope. Toward a Humanized Technology*, New York (American Mental Health Foundation) 2010, p. 9.

[4] Quoted in "Personal Responsibility Waning, Experts Say". Steven Thomma, Knight Ridder Newspapers, April 12, 2005

[5] David A. Zimmerman, *Deliver Us From Me-Ville*, Published by David C Cook, June 1, 2008. p. 32

[6] Brennen Manning, *Abba's Child*, NavPress, September 5, 2002

[7] Quoted in the book "Hand Me Another Brick" by Chuck Swindoll. Thomas Nelson, 1978. p. 82-83

[8] Larry Crabb, *Shattered Dreams*, WaterBrook Press, November 2, 2010

[9] Erwin McManus, *Chasing Daylight*, Thomas Nelson, January 10, 2006, p. 59

[10] Max Lucado, *Fearless Small Group Discussion Guide*, Thomas Nelson, 2009

[11] Peter Scazzerio, *Emotionally Healthy Spirituality*, Thomas Nelson, July 25, 2006, p. 120-121

[12] Henri Nouwen, *The Inner Voice of Love: A Journey Through Anguish to Freedom*, Image Books, January 19, 1999

[13] Isaiah 40:31 *King James Bible*, Zondervan, March 15, 2004

Acknowledgements

John Donne once wrote, "No man is an island, entire of itself; every man is a piece of the continent, a part of the main." His statement never rings truer than when you're going through the process of writing a book. So this is my opportunity to offer a token of thanks to the people I'm privileged to be connected with who have helped shape the words and offered support behind the scenes.

To my Mom to who this book is also dedicated: even as a writer I find it hard to find the words to express the gratitude I feel for all of the love, support and guidance you've given me. You've always been my biggest cheerleader and there's no way I would be able to do what I do without you.

To my family, Opa, Erin & John, Trevor & Hannah, Timmy, my aunts, uncles and many cousins: I feel very fortunate to be a part of such an amazing family that sticks together because, after all, the Muppets never leave a man behind. Special thanks to Auntie Denise & Uncle John for letting me retreat to your little piece of paradise to reflect, re-connect with God and write this book.

To my friends: I am so grateful for you and the steadfast support you've given me. My life would be a lot less richer without each one of you in it.

To my First Baptist Church family: I feel blessed to be a part of a group of people who love Jesus like you do and always welcome me with open arms.

To Pastor Gary and Wendy: without your support and assistance this book would have never made it off my laptop and into print. Thank you for encouraging me to use my gifts and for using yours to help me on this publishing journey.

To all of those who helped me to get my first book *Walking Through A Fallen World* out there and who have supported both my writing and radio ministry. Special thanks to the team at Harmony House, CHIM, LIFE 100.3 and all of the radio stations who air the MAD Christian Radio Show.

To Pastor Darryl: for faithfully guiding me on my journey through the wilderness and for never being more than a phone call away.

To Carole: for always going above and beyond the call of friendship, I'm so thankful to have you in my life and very much appreciate your help in editing this book.

To all of you who have faithfully lifted me up with prayer, words of encouragement, and support: you know who you are, thank you.

Finally, and most importantly, my deepest gratitude goes go God, the author of life and the One who gives and takes away: thank you for Your love, the grace You continually show me and for writing my name in Your story of Redemption.

About the Author

Kristen McNulty is the author of *Walking Through A Fallen World* and *Closed Doors*. She has also contributed to the books *True: Volume 2 (Zondervan)* and *P.S. I Love You – 52 Messages of Encouragement*. Kristen's writing has appeared in RELEVANT Magazine, RELEVANT Leader, Pulpit Helps, The Storyteller, eNcounter, and on numerous websites.

She is the host and producer of the MAD Christian Radio Show, a syndicated program aired on radio stations around the world and the winner of two American Christian Music Awards.

Kristen calls Timmins, Ontario home where she runs a website design business, Jumpstart Media. In her free time, she loves to write, read, take photos, go fishing, travel, play sports, spend time with friends and family, and explore the great outdoors.

Learn more and connect with Kristen at kristenmcnulty.com, email kristen@kristenmcnulty.com or scan the QR Code below with your phone.

www.ingramcontent.com/pod-product-compliance
Lightning Source LLC
Chambersburg PA
CBHW032040290426
44110CB00012B/887